LOST
OHIO
TREASURE

⚓ LOST ⚓
OHIO
TREASURE

MARK STRECKER

THE
History
PRESS

Published by The History Press
Charleston, SC
www.historypress.com

Front cover, top: "Ohio." Aaron Arrowsmith and Samuel Lewis, 1805. *Library of Congress Map Division*; *bottom*: General Armstrong, 1838–56. *Library of Congress. Back cover*: *Government Counterfeit Detector. New York Public Library Digital Collections.*

First published 2024

Manufactured in the United States

ISBN 9781467155908

Library of Congress Control Number: 20234949568

Notice: The information in this book is true and complete to the best of our knowledge. It is offered without guarantee on the part of the author or The History Press. The author and The History Press disclaim all liability in connection with the use of this book.

CONTENTS

ACKNOWLEDGEMENTS

I'd like the thank the following people for their help: Tim Sanders, Reference Department, Bossard Memorial Library, Gallipolis, Ohio; Randy Bergdorf, director/fiscal officer, Peninsula Library and Historical Society; Terry Metter, subject department librarian, Cleveland Public Library; Kelly Schroeder, local history and reference librarian, Putnam County District Library; Mark Moore, senior subject librarian, Cleveland Public Library; Terry Metter, subject department librarian, Cleveland Public Library; and those exceedingly helpful researchers on the Facebook group "Marquette and Bessemer No. 2," which was created by Captain Robert McLeod's descendants. Those who replied to my queries gave me invaluable information and pointed me to sources of which I wasn't aware. I especially want to thank Shaun Vary from that group, who tracked down some important bits of information.

AUTHOR'S NOTE

Unless otherwise noted, all geographical locations in this book are in Ohio. If a place is out of state, its location will only be reported the first time it appears in a chapter. Like so many rules, there are a few exceptions. When the location briefly moves to California, as an example, the reader will have no trouble recognizing that San Francisco and Sacramento are located in that state and not in Ohio. The same holds true for iconic cities such as New Orleans and New York City. The same goes for this book's index.

INTRODUCTION

The inspiration for this book is the television series *Expedition Unknown* and shows like it that spend each episode looking for a lost treasure based on clues from the historical record. The treasure is never found. With that in mind, I decided to look at some of Ohio's lost treasure stories to determine if there's any truth to them or not. I didn't have to dig very deep to figure out that for the most part, they're all fictitious.

Then I realized it didn't matter anyway. Treasure stories are an excellent gateway to history, a way to show that things that happened in the past can be just as compelling as a blockbuster thriller. The story about gold and silver buried during the French and Indian War, for example, involves skirmishes, battles and the death of a veteran British general. There are also a couple appearances by George Washington, who at that time was a lieutenant colonel in the Virginia militia. He led the men who fired the first shots of the French and Indian War, which was part of the Seven Years' War.

Equally interesting is the history of treasure hunting in America itself. Much of it is derived from European folklore and filled with a belief in magic. In the eighteenth and nineteenth centuries, numerous con artists exploited these superstitions for their own profit. In the twentieth century, hustlers replaced divining rods, fortunetelling and seer stones with dubious "scientific" instruments designed to find everything from oil and natural gas to gold. The first device that really could find hidden treasure was the metal detector. Its modern form was invented in the mid-1920s, and with it, detectorists have found all sorts of buried historical artifacts such as dog tags lost by World War II soldiers passing through Ohio.

Then there is real buried treasure uncovered purely by chance. I found a number of newspaper articles about buried money being found by accident in Ohio, often during the remodeling of a house or the demolition of one. There's a good reason for this. Until the bank reforms of the New Deal, Americans distrusted these institutions, and rightly so. They often failed, leaving depositors with nothing. As a result, people hid or buried their money and then either forgot about it or died before telling somewhere else where it was.

Chapter 1

THE TREASURE-SEEKING RACKET AND REAL TREASURE FOUND

The first Europeans who came to America brought with them their treasure-hunting superstitions, a belief system that made its way west into the Northwest Territory from which Ohio was carved. Some held that supernatural forces protected buried treasure that could be found only by those skilled enough to deal with them. Treasure hunters employed all sorts of mystical means, including magical tomes, soothsayers, mirrors (a favorite of those of German heritage) and seer stones. This last item came in all shapes and sizes and was considered special because it had something unusual about it.

Buried treasure often had guardian spirits that came in a variety of forms, including the ghosts of murdered youths and Indigenous people. The best time to dig it up was between midnight and sunrise. In New England, it was believed the spirits of Black pirates guarded Captain Kidd's buried treasure. Such guardians were clever and often outright terrifying, coming in the form of a headless man riding a black horse (sound familiar?) or shooting blue flames into the sky. Diggers believed they needed absolute silence to sneak up on a guardian. When they failed to find the treasure, they presumed that the guardian had moved it.

Dreams and fortunetellers were another way of finding lost treasure. In August 1880, a man living in Richland County dreamed of a kettle filled with gold that was supposedly buried by Native Americans on Bishop's Farm. A consultation with a fortuneteller in Bucyrus fortified his resolve. He sought

"Ways of Using a Divining Rod." Bain News Service. *Library of Congress.*

the help of a man named Kline who had a divining rod, the employment of which goes back to at least the ancient Greeks, who invented the word *rhabdomancy* to describe its use. News of the man's dream spread, prompting John Fry, Joseph Bishop, James Corrothers and John Cole to buy Bishop's Farm and begin hunting for the kettle. Kline and his divining rod made a systematic search of the grounds. At the spot where it indicated something was buried, the four men began excavating. Finding nothing, they realized they'd been fools to believe in the treasure.

In the 1890s, eastern Ohio experienced an oil and natural gas boom. This attracted fraudsters with divining rods claiming they could find undiscovered deposits. One such person got his fee whether he succeeded or not. His rod, if one can call it that, consisted of two wires shaped into a crude fork on which he placed a cap filled with some secret substance. The rod wiggled for him, but when a bystander tried it, he couldn't reproduce the same effect. The diviner claimed that he'd "found enough gas to blow up the whole country," but when a shaft was sunk, it hit only water.

In 1881, a fortuneteller calling himself Dr. George Schmidt arrived in Cleveland. On September 11 of that year, Louisa Kneis went to him to have her future told. Schmidt reported that in 1751, slaveowners had buried a treasure worth $1 million in her door-yard. He'd come to Cleveland specifically to see her. He had the power of the Divine Being and was a prophet of the Divine One—whatever those were. He received his messages from a higher power. The treasure on her land, he warned, was guarded by Satan himself. To show just how serious he was, he showed her a copy of his magical tome, *The Sixth and Seventh Books of Moses*.

This book, still in print, is just one of many found throughout history claiming Moses as its author. Two papyri from around the fourth century CE were known as the *Eighth (or Holy) Book of Moses*, and these mentioned the existence of lost books penned by Moses that didn't make it into the Bible. A book titled *Harba de-Moshe*, or *Sword of Moses*, appeared in Europe during the Renaissance. In it one could find, wrote Owen Davies in his book *Grimoires: A History of Magic Books*, "practical magical recipes written in a mix of Hebrew, Aramaic and gibberish."

In 1725, a book printed in Cologne, Germany, purported to contain more lost works of Moses. The *Sixth and Seventh Books of Moses* surfaced in Germany in the nineteenth century. Its first English edition appeared in 1880. No one knows who wrote it. One legend claims that an early copy was once stored in Wittenberg, Germany, the city where Martin Luther wrote his famous theses. In the 1860s, Americans started making paper of wood pulp, allowing for much cheaper books. As a result, low-cost copies of the *Sixth and Seventh Books of Moses* selling for one dollar flooded the U.S. market.

Schmidt told Kneis that he'd fight Satan to secure the treasure for a mere $600. Not having that much on her, she gave him $50 as a down payment. The next day, she mortgaged her house through Wick and Company to raise the rest. Upon receiving his fee, Schmidt absconded from Cleveland. Authorities soon caught him and charged him with obtaining money under false pretenses.

In 1904, fortunetellers in Washingtonville—a village on the border of Mahoning and Columbiana Counties—claimed they knew of a lost fortune located in a seventy-five-year-old farmhouse not far out of town. It had once belonged to Captain Kidsim, a wealthy hermit who had vanished while traveling to Cleveland. After his disappearance, his house was purchased by Adam Stouffer, who willed it to his son, Frank. The people of Washingtonville pledged to investigate the matter.

During the Great Depression, magical instruments were replaced with a range of equally useless "scientific" gadgets claiming to find buried treasure. *Popular Mechanics* warned readers about some of these devices in its February 1937 article "The Buried Treasure Racket." The magazine's staff tried several of these devices, including the "scientific gold compass." Devices like it supposedly picked up vibrations given off by precious metals known as doodlebugs. To test this particular one, the magazine staff put vegetables and a few gold coins into six boxes. The compass chose a box containing a tomato.

A peddler of a device he called a "gold magnet" walked into the office of a businessman and claimed that his device could locate that precious metal. The peddler handed the businessman a gold watch and told him to hide it where he'd like. After the peddler left the room, "the businessman wrapped the watch in thick paper and placed it far back in a desk drawer." He cracked open a window to allow the sounds of the city to penetrate the office. When the peddler returned, the gold magnet consistently located the watch in a closet. The businessman had correctly concluded that the peddler located the watch by listening to its ticking, and the noise coming from outside ruined the scam.

One "treasure racketeer" had a device attached to the back of his car constructed from copper helixes and decorated with electrical instruments. He claimed his device could detect precious metals up to fifty miles away. He charged a fee for locating treasure, taking half before looking and half after it was dug up. He skedaddled before those doing the digging realized they'd been had. During the detecting phase, he zigged and zagged, then said he was within fifty feet of the treasure and that was as close as he could get. His con worked particularly well because a confederate met a mark ahead of time and ascertained where that person believed buried treasure might be located.

Something that can legitimately find objects hidden beneath the ground or water is a metal detector. During a search on an Ashtabula farm, one metal detectorist found an array of items including a 1942 wheat penny and Matchbox cars. Another unearthed a diamond bracelet valued at $7,200 at the time of its discovery. Most metal detectorists aren't looking to get rich but rather enjoy finding lost things. The Dayton Diggers use them to find historic artifacts. During their first venture on August 15, 2009, the Diggers found four Spanish reales—the equivalent of the American half dollar—as well as an 1825 penny.

Buried treasure is usually found by accident. In 1852, the son of Daniel Vantrees struck metal with his hoe at the roots of a fallen oak tree. He was working in a lot owned by Isaiah Totten from Fort Recovery. He unearthed a small wooden box containing nine hundred silver coins and Spanish doubloons worth around $14,000. Some thought this was the payroll buried during the Battle of the Wabash, a story local lore embellished with the claim that a man from Virginia supposedly came to Fort Recovery looking for it in 1818. He spent some time searching, and then one day, his body was discovered in the woods.

The Battle of the Wabash was the end of a failed military expedition led by Arthur St. Clair to deal with Ohio's hostile Native population, who had taken exception to Americans settling on their lands. At the time, St. Clair was both the Northwest Territory's governor and a general in the U.S. Army. President George Washington ordered him to march a force to the Maumee River and there build a fort near the villages of the Miami people. Despite poor health, St. Clair obeyed. At Fort Washington near Cincinnati, he assembled a small a force of regulars supplemented by a poorly trained, ill-disciplined militia. His little army headed north on September 17, 1791. The farther it went, the more men from its militia portion deserted, mostly because of insufficient rations.

St. Clair ordered 300 of his regulars to pursue and capture the deserters, none of whom was found. This left him with just 1,400 men, who were attacked on November 4 at the Wabash River by a coalition of Native Americans led by Mihsihkinaahkwa (Little Turtle) and Weyapiersenwah (Blue Jacket). A staggering 647 Americans were killed and 280 wounded;

Major General Arthur St. Clair. *New York Public Library Digital Collections.*

30 female camp followers were also killed and mutilated. It was during the fighting that St. Clair supposedly had the army's payroll buried. General Anthony Wayne returned to the spot in 1794 to build Fort Recovery, from which the present-day village takes its name.

St. Clair had much trouble gathering sufficient supplies for the expedition. The idea that he had a payroll of gold that he pointlessly took with him into the wilderness is absurd. It's more likely the cache of coins unearthed by Vantrees were someone's savings hidden away for safekeeping and then forgotten about. That's what happened to a man living in Belmont County. During or shortly after the Civil War, his house was robbed. His wife decided it best to hide their remaining wealth, so she stashed bundles each worth $400 or $500 in various places in and around the house. She told no one, not even her husband, where she'd put them, and that knowledge died with her. Sometime after she passed, her husband hired his son-in-law to clean out the smokehouse. There the son-in-law and a hired assistant dug up about $400 worth of half dollars.

Harrison Damon died in the village of Hinckley in 1882. Over his lifetime, he'd amassed a considerable amount of wealth, including the sale of a tract of land for $3,000 paid in gold and silver. Distrusting banks, he hid his money in and around his house, never telling family or friends where it was. He once told his wife he had a total of $30,000 hidden away, and he pledged to one day tell her the locations so she and their children knew where to find it. A sudden apoplexy—probably a stroke—rendered him unconscious. He lingered in that state for several days before death took him. After his burial, the family found a memorandum book showing his savings amounted to $33,500.

The family searched for the money but found nothing. Needing it to live, the widow prayed that the location would be located. She felt compelled to visit the beehives kept near the house and there found $15,000 in greenbacks. One afternoon, a young man dropped his keys in her barn, forcing him to pry up a plank to get them. Below he found a half-gallon fruit jar containing $20 gold pieces. Further searching unearthed five more jars filled with $5 and $10 coins. A two-bushel grain bag on the opposite side of the barn contained silver. This along with the dollars amounted to $23,000.

In late October 1898, Oscar Osborne of Richfield was found dead with a strap around his neck. Authorities ruled his death homicide and speculated that the killer had used the strap in an effort to get Osborne to tell where he'd hidden his money. It was common knowledge that Osborne had a small fortune hidden somewhere in his house. A few weeks earlier, he'd told a neighbor where the stash was located, so after his death, the neighbor recovered $10,000 in money.

In July 1901, during the demolition of a brick house built in the first decade of the 1800s, workers in the village of Calcutta found a rusted box in the stone foundation. Within were copper and silver coins dating no later than 1810, with most having a mint date from the previous century. The cache contained mainly English coins, with a few from France and Spain mixed in.

Most caches of wealth dating from the late eighteenth and early nineteenth centuries consisted of foreign coins because at that time they were legal tender in the United States. In 1792, Congress created a U.S. decimal monetary system based on the Spanish silver dollar and authorized the creation of an American currency. A lack of sufficient gold and silver meant that minting coins in the quantity needed was not possible, so to compensate, foreign coins were made a legal medium of exchange.

During the Napoleonic Wars, America's already paltry supply of foreign coins (mostly Spanish) shrank considerably, with larger denominations disappearing altogether. Along the East Coast, small-value coins still circulated, but in the interior, they were made into cut money, which were coins sheered into smaller pieces. An 1831 report from a House committee noted that most of the money circulating in the United States was paper. Spanish gold dollars rarely circulated. The committee estimated that just $4 million in coins, most of it being underweight silver, circulated throughout the entire country.

Things briefly improved between 1834 and 1837, but the Panic of 1837 caused hard currency to disappear from circulation. In the early 1840s, the United States was forced to import more foreign coins. It wasn't until the early 1850s that it had a large enough supply of domestic coins in circulation to allow it to ban foreign ones as legal tender. The federal government issued its first national paper currency during the Civil War, and from that point on, this form of money became more acceptable and thus more likely to be hidden away than coins.

In 2016, a Cleveland couple renovating their house built in the 1940s found a green suitcase hidden in their basement's ceiling. Within were three bundles wrapped in what appeared to be wax paper under which was a *Cleveland Plain Dealer* newspaper dated March 25, 1951. The first package contained $20 bills, the second $50 bills and the third $100 bills. Also in the suitcase was a gold certificate as well as brown and star notes—improvised currency used in Hawaii during World War II. The cache was valued at about $23,000.

CHAPTER 2

NO TREASURE FOUND HERE

A number of lost treasure tales unearthed for this book turned out to be duds. The author found that if a lost treasure story contained specific directions or had a map pointing to the exact spot where the treasure was buried, this was a dead giveaway that the treasure didn't exist in the first place. Some of the stories the author looked at were "historical events" that never happened. Others were hoaxes based on real world events to give them a sheen of plausibility. All the tales of lost treasure in this chapter are stories that treasure hunters still share today.

In 1876, pirates on the Ohio River supposedly stole $24,000 worth of gold off a steamboat and buried their ill-gotten gains on a bluff overlooking the river roughly one mile northeast of Crown City in Gallia County. That they buried it instead of dividing it up immediately is a common characteristic of such stories. The fact that the steamboat in question isn't named makes it that much harder to track down. The author scoured newspaper accounts from 1876 and came up empty. He expanded his search to the entire decade of the 1870s and still found nothing. Undaunted, he contacted the Gallia County Bossard Memorial Library and asked if anyone there had heard of it. Reference librarian Tim Sanders told him that he, too, had looked into this and found nothing. Not only that, but the bluff in question doesn't exist, although it is possible construction done in the past eliminated it.

There is a similar tale in Lake County. In 1862, three men stole from a Canadian bank $50,000 or $100,000 worth of gold and then sailed across Lake Erie to Fairport Harbor with it. Shortly after landing, they fell out, and one killed the other two. The survivor buried the gold. A year or more later, he turned up in Chicago dying of either tuberculosis or pulmonary failure (sources vary). The robber told his doctor where he'd hidden his ill-gotten gains: "The gold is buried three feet deep, all the bars together, 20 paces northwest from a large oak tree near the west bank of the Grand River, in Ohio, about two miles south of the lake." The doctor went looking but found nothing. The author found no evidence of a robbery of that much gold occurring anywhere in Canada at a place where it borders Lake Erie in 1862 or any other year of the Civil War.

Often treasure stories are exaggerations or misunderstandings of actual events. A good example is the wreck of the Lake Shore & Michigan Southern Railroad's *Pacific Express* train. On the night of December 29, 1876, a collapsed bridge spanning a deep gully caused all but the train's lead locomotive to plummet sixty-nine feet onto the frozen Ashtabula River below. Many of those who survived the fall perished in fires started by tipped-over heating stoves.

Because of the snowstorm and the difficulty to get to the wreck site, it was for a time left unguarded, allowing thieves to move in. One wealthy young man lay there with four broken ribs and a gash to his head. Near him were his dead mother and sister. Two men lifted him up awkwardly, causing pain so intense it knocked him unconscious. From his person, thieves stole a present from his father and two purses, one containing about fifty dollars and the other some dollars and his mother's jewelry. When he awoke, the only valuable left to him was a watch he'd hidden among his clothes. The thieves had even taken his train ticket for California.

Other victims—both alive and dead—were similarly robbed. Items taken included diamond pins, watches and jewels. Trunks were plundered. A man who made it to the nearby Eagle Hotel was robbed of $300 there. The next morning, rescuers descended on the wreck site and found scattered diamonds and a melted gold watch. The train was supposedly carrying $2 million in gold bullion. The author found nothing in the historic record to verify this. Even if true, surely its owner would have made every effort to recover it. The gold bullion story is probably an exaggerated version of the fact that some lost valuables were made of gold that was melted by the fires, some of which may well be at the bottom of the Ashtabula River waiting to be found by someone with a metal detector.

Such distortions of what happened are a frequent occurrence with treasure stories. The numerous stories about lost Shawnee silver mines are a good example. They can all be traced to a January 1917 article written by

THE OLD BRIDGE.
[From a Photograph by T. T. Sweeny, Cleveland.]

This illustration of the Ashtabula train bridge that collapsed is from a photograph by T.T. Sweeny of Cleveland. *From* The Ashtabula Disaster *by Stephen D. Peet, 1877. Digitized by Google Books.*

Professor R.S. King that appeared in the *Ohio Archeological and Historical Society Quarterly.* King made it clear at the outset that no silver mines ever existed in Ohio, and what he was about to relate was a story told to him by his father, who was born and raised in Greene County.

Early pioneers who settled in the Northwest Territory were sometimes captured by the Shawnees and taken to their town of Old Chillicothe, a place where modern Oldtown now stands. In the morning, Shawnees would blindfold their prisoners at this place and then march them three to three and a half miles up Massies Creek, where they were guarded for about a half day. During this time, some of the Shawnees went elsewhere.

When they returned, they had with them bundles of a weight far heavier than their size would indicate. Prisoners had to carry these loads back to Old Chillicothe without being given a chance to rest. One of the prisoners worked his blindfold down far enough that he could see. He reported that none of the Shawnees left as thought, but rather spent the day digging up silver out of a mine. Because this eyewitness was a known liar, no one believed him.

In 1780, American general George Rogers Clark launched a punitive expedition against the Shawnee people. As he closed in on Old Chillicothe

in Greene County, Chief Catecahassa (Black Hoof) ordered that all silver and other valuables were to be gathered up and buried. The Shawnees burned the town as they departed and then headed for Piqua, where some of the silver was buried. Rogers attacked Piqua, at which the Shawnee warriors manned a triangular fort. Repeated fire by a brass cannon forced the Shawnee fighters to retreat. It's said a ton or more of silver was placed in a pit, covered with brush and burned. The rest was buried in a hole along the Little Miami River. Isaac Zane, who was captured by Wyandots at the age of nine, claimed to know about it.

Opposite: This lithograph of Payta-Kootha (Flying Clouds) by John T. Bowen is an example of what a Shawnee warrior looked like. *Library of Congress.*

Right: George Rogers Clark. *New York Public Library Digital Collections.*

Another Shawnee silver story involved land purchased by James Stevenson on which flowed Massies Creek. Stevenson had moved from Kentucky to Ohio in 1796 or 1797. He sold this land to his son-in-law, Vincent King, who built a flour mill on it. While digging a race along the creek, several stones were unearthed containing symbols on them. Men who'd heard the tale of the silver mine believed the stones proved the mine was at this spot, so here they started digging. They gave up upon striking water.

Just like Shawnee silver mines, there is no truth to the story that Andrew John Baldwin built his tavern in Lancaster using plunder taken during his time as a pirate under the command of Captain Jean Lafitte in the Gulf of Mexico. Lafitte was a smuggler, pirate and privateer best known for aiding Andrew Jackson during the Battle of New Orleans. Baldwin, who built his tavern in 1818, was said to accept only gold coins for business transactions. This is plausible because many Americans rightly distrusted paper money issued by banks. To increase his already considerable fortune, Baldwin allegedly murdered guests at his inn on occasion and then buried their property somewhere on his land. After his death in 1840, treasure hunters are said to have located a cache of gold in a hollowed-out stone in his barn's attic.

Nothing about Baldwin's past suggests he made his way to the Gulf of Mexico and served as a pirate. Born in Virginia in 1861, he lived for a time in Adams County, Pennsylvania. Captain Lafitte was active as a pirate between 1810 and 1823, meaning Baldwin was between forty-nine and fifty-six during Lafitte's career. This made him far too old to work on a pirate ship. Most pirates were in their twenties because sailors of the day needed the stamina and physical strength of youth to perform the arduous duties of working a sailing ship.

So where did the story that Baldwin had been a pirate come from? An Irish nobleman who visited Baldwin's inn wrote about him in a travel book, and it's he who made the spurious claim that Baldwin and two of his brothers had served under Captain Lafitte. John Baldwin died on August 14, 1840, leaving 180 acres of land to his older brother Francis and more possessions to other heirs. Baldwin's house, built in 1820, stood close to Lancaster where Pleasant and Marietta Roads meet. It was demolished in 1951.

While rumors of Baldwin's possible criminal activities are undoubtedly all false, there can be no doubt that the Morgantown Gang operated mainly in Beaver Township, which was then in Columbiana County. The gang repeatedly broke the law over many years. According to the treasure story associated with them, they operated around East Liverpool, a town along the Ohio River where they kept their ill-gotten gains in two shacks. Fed up, authorities rounded up the gang members. All were found guilty and sent to prison. When they got out, police kept such close tabs on them that none dared to recover their loot.

Azariah Paulin started the gang during the Civil War. He and his family were all Copperheads—Southern sympathizers—and it's they who made up the Morgantown Gang's core. Paulin's farm was called Morgantown in honor of Confederate general John Morgan, who boldly invaded Ohio in the summer of 1863 (see chapter 7). The Morgantown Gang terrorized the community around them for about twenty years with crimes that included perjury, arson and theft.

So adept was Paulin at keeping authorities from gathering sufficient evidence to convict him or members of his gang in a criminal trial that he was dubbed the "Old Fox" or "Old Chief." He had a farm near Steamtown in Noble County. Around 1880, neighbor Thomas Campbell started a berry patch on Paulin's land in exchange for splitting the profits fifty-fifty. Shortly before its harvest, Paulin forbade Campbell from stepping on his land. He kept all the money made from the crop's sales for himself, causing Campbell to lose between $1,200 and $1,500. This incident prompted authorities to finally rid the area of the Morgantown Gang, an effort that took three years.

"The Soldier's Song—Unionism vs. Copperheadism." Smith & Swinney, 1864. *Library of Congress.*

On July 15, 1883, Morgantown Gang members Simon Paulin, Bill Cluse and Jacob Paulin burned down the house of Jacob Buzzard. For this they were arrested. At the trial, Simon pleaded guilty and the other two were found guilty. Two of Paulin's sons, George and Charles, went on the run. Changing their names to Charles Reed and George Williams, they claimed to have come from Pennsylvania and had previously worked as teachers in Youngstown. They went to work for a mining company at Mineral Point (now Mineral City) in Tuscarawas County. In early August 1884, a marshal from a neighboring town arrested them. George was convicted of perjury and sentenced to three years in prison.

In mid-1884, Azariah was charged with arson, perjury, concealing stolen property and corrupting witnesses. Given a bail of $2,200, he mortgaged his farm to pay for it. Released on July 24, he went on the run around January 5, 1885. Mahoning County sheriff Eli B. Walker spent the next several months tracking him. Paulin was apprehended in Shippensburg, Pennsylvania, by Constable Armon and none other than Thomas Campbell, the neighbor whom Paulin had cheated. Paulin had just $7 or $8 on his person. At his trial, Paulin pleaded guilty to sending his men to burn down Jacob Buzzard's house. He was also found guilty for the subordination of a jury and sentenced to three years in prison.

If the gang had any ill-gotten gains stashed in a couple of shacks along the Ohio, it is unlikely any remained after serving their prison sentences. Surely Azariah would have grabbed any hidden loot before jumping bail. Also, why would he mortgage his farm if had a considerable number of assets elsewhere? The idea that law enforcement could keep such a close watch on gang members after their release from prison that they were unable to elude them is absurd. No rural county law enforcement agency in America at the time had the manpower, ability or financial resources to tail all the former members of the gang until they died. And even if they did, someone not under their watch could have retrieved the gang's hidden wealth.

Chapter 3

BURIED FRENCH GOLD

In 1829, a stranger from North Carolina arrived in East Rochester. The precise month or day is, like so many aspects of this tale, not recorded. He brought with him a letter written in French that he'd found among his uncle's papers detailing where a cache of French gold and silver coins was buried. An April 14, 1881 article in the *Stark County Democrat* reported that the treasure could be found using the following landmarks: a "rock-hill side, opposite a certain spring; [a] deer cut on a tree; three springs, one half mile south; [and] stones in the forks of a tree." The stranger asked locals to tell him where these places could be found. Despite his offered bribes of money or his horse's bridle and saddle, he got no answers. The locals knew these locations but kept that knowledge to themselves with plans to look for the treasure on their own.

The stranger's uncle had, the story goes, served in the French army during the French and Indian War. He was stationed at Fort Duquesne, which stood on the spot where the Allegheny and the Monongahela Rivers meet to form the Ohio River—the place where Pittsburgh, Pennsylvania, now stands. With the British army closing in, a decision was made to send all the fort's wealth back to Canada. A contingent of ten men took it out on the backs of sixteen mules and headed north by northwest. The British pursued.

Just before the British caught up with and attacked the mule train, the French buried their cache at a place that later became George Robbins's farm near East Rochester. Only two French soldiers, the stranger's uncle and Henri Muselle, survived that day. The uncle reported that before departing, he carved the picture of a deer into a tree just east of the hole. The French hid their shovels, and these were supposedly found later by treasure hunters.

The reason for the British attack on Fort Duquesne can be traced back to 1749, when Pierre-Joseph Céleron de Bienville led an expedition into the Ohio country and claimed it for the French crown. During his excursion, he visited Logstown (called Chiningue by the French), a village consisting mainly of Shawnees and Lenapes (Delawares) with a smattering of Cayugas, Miamis and Mohawks. It was located near present-day Baden, Pennsylvania. Bienville discovered that British traders had established a firm foothold here, threatening France's lucrative fur trade. This intelligence made its way back to France, prompting it to order Canada's governor-general, Michel-Ange Duquesne de Menneville, the Marquis Duquesne, and Canada's intendant, François Bigot, to drive British traders out of the Ohio country while at the same time making peace with its Indigenous people.

Duquesne was born in about 1700 in Toulon, France. He came from a military and naval family of Huguenots. After joining the French Royal Navy, he converted to Catholicism because Protestants couldn't rise very high in rank in that service. Unable to purchase commissions, he earned all of his promotions based on merit and ability, which one day allowed him to achieve the rank of rear admiral. His first visit to Canada occurred early in his naval career during his service on the ship *Élephant*. Here she ran aground and then suffered from the indignity of being plundered by salvagers.

Duquesne was appointed Canada's governor-general in 1751 and arrived in Quebec on July 1, 1752. One of his first acts was to instill discipline in the regular troops and militia, a foreshadowing of what was to come. He relied on Canada's intendant, Bigot, to oversee the colony's civil authority, which included financial matters and the administration of justice. The intendant's job was to make sure the colonial government was run effectively. This office was created by King Louis XIV in 1663, and the man who filled it was Canada's second highest-ranking official.

Bigot, who was born in Bordeaux, France, was baptized on January 30, 1703. He made a career in financial management working for the French government. A notorious gambler who made sure to put personal profit before duty, he was sent to work in Canada twice, a place not to his liking and from which he desperately wanted to be recalled. He first traveled there in May 1739 to serve as Cape Breton Island's financial commissioner.

Returning home in 1745, he was appointed Canada's intendant three years later, requiring him to relocate to Quebec. His instructions put a special emphasis on helping the governor-general expand French control of North America. Later, when the French lost the Seven Years' War and with it all of Canada, blame for this was placed on colonial officials. Bigot, still intendant, was among the scapegoats. Officials sent him to the Bastille for two years on trumped-up fraud charges. Upon his release, he was exiled from France for life.

In 1752, he and Governor Duquesne made plans to send a military force south to eject the troublesome British traders, a plan opposed by the colonial army's officers. That October, the governor announced he would send a force of 300 regulars and 1,700 militiamen under the command of sixty-one-year-old Paul Marin de la Malgue to the upper part of the Ohio River to construct and garrison a series of forts. The Malgue expedition departed in the spring of 1753. Malgue pushed himself hard during the summer and spring, arresting British traders along the way and nearly starving his men. Clearly ill, he refused to take time off to rest, preferring instead to die in the field. Which he did on October 29 at Fort de la Rivière au Boeuf, located in what is now Waterford, Pennsylvania.

The first person Duquesne asked to replace Malgue declined, so he named Captain Claude-Pierre Pécaudy de Contrecoeur to take command. Stationed at Fort Niagara, Contrecoeur was a professional soldier. He didn't like to be away from his family in Quebec, where he was born on December 28, 1705, but he had no choice. Tasked with building a fort at Logstown, he took a detachment of thirty men with him there. Finding it devoid of the lumber needed for a fort's construction, he abandoned the site.

In April 1754, Contrecoeur led his men down the Alleghany River where it met the Monongahela River to form the Ohio River. Here he found forty-one Virginians under the command of Edward Ward building a fort. The British called this location the Forks or the Point. Contrecoeur asked the British to leave in peace, which they did on April 16, 1754. He bought the Virginians' tools and constructed the French fort by building on what they had already built. He named the fort in honor of Governor Duquesne. It was designed to hold a garrison of two hundred to three hundred men. Its firepower consisted of eight small cannons plus the muskets of those within.

As the exiled British builders made their way home, they happened upon a Virginian militia headed to the Forks to reinforce them. The militia's leader, Lieutenant Colonel George Washington of Mount Vernon, Virginia, knew he didn't have the strength to confront the French, so he wrote to his commanders informing them of the situation. Receiving news on May 24 that a detached French force had crossed the Youghiogheny River about

Above: This portrait of a young Lieutenant Colonel George Washington by Charles Willson Peale was painted in 1772, some twenty years after he first held this rank. *Wikimedia Commons.*

Opposite: Fort Necessity Stockyard at Great Meadows. Fort Necessity National Battlefield, Farmington, Pennsylvania. *Photo by the author.*

eighteen miles away, Washington decided to move his men to the Great
Meadows near present-day Uniontown, Pennsylvania.

On May 27, Seneca chief Tanaghrisson sent Washington intelligence
that a French detachment under the command of Ensign Joseph Coulon
de Villiers was camped at what is now called Jumonville Glen, a place about
three miles east of present-day Hopwood, Pennsylvania. Tanaghrisson,
who lived in Logstown, had reluctantly allied himself with the British with
the hope they'd help him push the French out of Iroquois lands. It was he
who'd suggested the British build a fort at the Forks, and he and some of his
warriors had been there when Contrecoeur arrived.

Early the next morning, Washington and his men alongside Tanaghrisson
and his warriors attacked the French at Jumonville Glen. The French
surrendered after a fifteen-minute skirmish. This is considered the opening
shots of the French and Indian War, which was part of the Seven Years' War.
Ten French soldiers died and around twenty-one were captured. Tanaghrisson
may have killed the wounded Villiers with a tomahawk *after* the French
surrendered. Upon hearing of this fight, Contrecoeur sent a large force to
track down and capture Washington and his men. Washington decided to
make a stand at Great Meadows, where he ordered the construction of Fort
Necessity. He surrendered after a daylong battle.

He was told he could go home so long as he pledged not to return to the area for a year and a day. A document to that effect was drafted. Unknown to Washington, the French version contained the word "assassination," this implying that Washington had murdered Villers. Washington later said had he known the word "assassination" was in the document, he'd never have signed it. It's probable that his interpreter, Jacob Van Braam, unintentionally mistranslated the word into English as something less provocative. Van Braam had an imperfect understanding of English.

Fort Duquesne's garrison was briefly increased to 1,500 men after the incident at Fort Necessity and then reduced to a more manageable 500. Contrecoeur wanted to return to Quebec to be with his family, so in the fall of 1754, Governor Duquesne ordered the forty-four-year-old Captain Daniel-Hyacinthe-Marie Liénard de Beaujeu to replace him.

The British Crown laid claim to much of the land the French now occupied. King George II had little interest in a military confrontation with the French, but the battle at Fort Necessity prompted the British cabinet to act. It decided to send two regiments of foot soldiers from Ireland to North America. Major General Edward Braddock was given command of all North American forces. He and the regiments departed from Cork, Ireland, on January 15, 1755. They landed at Hampton Roads, Virginia, in March.

Born in 1695, Braddock joined the British army on August 29, 1710, and spent the rest of his life serving in it. Around sixty when he sailed for America, his appointment as commander-in-chief generated gossip. Some said he'd gotten it because he was a favorite of the king, others that he'd begged for the position so he could pay off his gambling debts. With no known portraits of Braddock painted during his lifetime, the best description of him says he was short and grew fat in his last years. He had a temper and was a strict disciplinarian.

He found nothing but disorganization in Virginia. Leaders from different colonies disagreed with one another, a problem amplified by petty jealousies. Magazines hadn't been filled and promised militias not raised. Braddock found the British army regulars already stationed in the colonies undesirable. He decided to launch separate attacks against the French forts in the Canadian province of Nova Scotia as well as ones in what is today the state of New York: Crown Point and Niagara. He would personally lead a campaign against Fort Duquesne.

He assembled the army for the expedition at Fort Cumberland, Maryland. By incorporating colonial militia into his army, he was able to

Above: Map of the French and Indian War, by James McConnell, 1919. *Library of Congress Map Division.*

Left: This engraving by William Sartain of General Edward Braddock was published around 1899 and is pure conjecture: no likeness of him is known to have been made during his lifetime. *Library of Congress.*

increase its total size to about 2,400. He had a daunting task ahead of him. Fort Duquesne stood about 220 miles away. To get to it, his army needed to cross forest-covered mountains where no roads yet existed. Needing local knowledge, he asked George Washington to be one of his aides-de-camp. Somewhat hesitantly because it was planting season at Mount Vernon, Washington agreed and headed to Fort Cumberland. He suggested that Braddock's force should travel light and fight like the Indigenous people, but the old general was having none of that. Braddock decided to build a road to accommodate the vast number of wagons he envisioned using, most of which he failed to acquire.

His army set out on June 8. Bogged down with twenty-nine guns and a hefty number of supplies, it moved exceedingly slow. Engineers built a road roughly that followed Nemacolin's Path, Nemacolin being a Lenape chief. Using hand tools and gunpowder coupled with human, equine and bovine muscle, Braddock's engineers cut a road twelve feet wide that stretched 110 miles. Washington urged Braddock to detach a lightly equipped column of men to move ahead. To this the general agreed, and he personally led the detachment of 1,400 men that brought with it artillery and supply wagons.

The detachment was within a few miles of Fort Duquesne on July 6. At about ten o'clock in the morning on that day, Braddock's Native American scouts returned, one of them carrying the scalp of a Frenchman. They reported that the French hadn't modified their fort, nor did they have any pickets posted. That same day, a skirmish against French-allied Native Americans erupted. During the fight, a British soldier mistakenly shot and killed the scout who'd brought the scalp back. The British stopped their march to bury this victim of friendly fire.

Beaujeu reached Fort Duquesne just as the British closed in. Aware of the size of Braddock's force and the British general's clear intention of laying siege, Beaujeu could see he didn't stand a chance. With just a few cannons, the fort's garrison of two hundred men supplemented by about eight hundred Native American allies living outside Duquesne's walls in bark sheds and wigwams wasn't going to repel the British for long.

So far as he and Contrecoeur were concerned, they could either make a token resistance and surrender, or they could burn the fort and retreat. One of their subordinates, Captain Jean-Daniel Dumas, had other ideas. Originally from Montauban, France, he was born on February 24, 1721. He joined the French army in 1742 and fought in the War of Austrian Succession. He'd arrived in Canada in 1750 and became a skilled negotiator with the Indigenous people of Acadia.

He argued that they should attack the British before they reached the fort, gaining time for reinforcements to arrive. His Native American allies were less enthusiastic, and most declined to participate because they incorrectly believed the British force had as many as 4,000 men. On the morning of July 9, 1755, Beaujeu and Dumas led 192 Canadians and 637 Indigenous allies composed of Lenapes, Wyandots and some Abenakis. Contrecoeur and 100 men remained in the fort with the plan to burn it if Beaujeu and Dumas's delaying action failed.

When the British reached a place called Little Meadows near present-day Grantsville, Maryland, it became clear the wagons could go no farther. A force of 1,200 men and ten cannons pressed ahead to lay siege on the fort. At eleven o'clock in the morning or noon on July 9, a column of 300 men, a company of grenadiers and two cannons led by Lieutenant Colonel Thomas Gage went to secure a spot where the main force would cross the Monongahela River. It's here the French attacked.

A brief European-style battle erupted in which Beaujeu was killed by the third volley of British artillery. Captain Dumas counterattacked alongside his Indigenous allies. Gage's men, already spooked by the horror stories of what Native American warriors did to those whites they captured, ran back to the main force. Dumas and his allies pursued. When they came across Braddock and his army, they attacked from behind trees, rendering British cannons ineffective.

The British retreated three or four times. Braddock kept trying to rally his men and had four horses shot from under him before a bullet pierced his lung, causing British resistance to crumble. Panicked wagon drivers drove away. This is the spark for yet another treasure tale associated with Fort Duquesne, which goes like this: one of the wagons carried the army payroll consisting of $25,000 English gold coins. It was taken to and buried where present-day Minerva stands.

This story can be dismissed as pure fiction. Before leaving on the expedition, Braddock promised privates in his army heading into the wilderness that they'd receive an extra sixpence a day, drummers ninepence and sergeants a shilling, but no one would receive *any* money until they returned to Philadelphia. On the march there'd be no use for ready money because in the wilderness there was nothing available to buy except illegal whiskey at their camp in the mountains.

The historical records tell us that during the retreat, about sixty British soldiers were killed or wounded. The officers did their best to maintain order. Braddock died on July 13. He was buried under the road so wagons driving

DEFEAT OF GENERAL BRADDOCK, IN THE FRENCH AND INDIAN WAR, IN VIRGINIA, IN 1755.

John T. Andrews. "Braddock's Defeat," 1855. *Library of Congress.*

over it would hide the grave from possible desecration. In 1823, workers constructing the National Road found it, robbing Braddock of his medals and other military paraphernalia as well as some of his bones. The rest of his remains were buried about one-fourth mile from the spot where Fort Necessity once stood. A marker was erected on this spot in 1913.

It was during the battle that the French supposedly sent a train of mules carrying gold and silver to Canada via an overland route across what is now the state of Ohio with a detachment of British soldiers in pursuit. Considering the disorder and panic that Braddock's force experienced during and after the battle, it's unlikely any officer could have induced soldiers to plunge deeper into the wilderness.

Perhaps that's why a few hunters of this elusive treasure argue that the mule train incident occurred during the second British attack on Fort Duquesne. At the beginning of 1758, things weren't going well for the British. To reverse its fortunes, Britain's secretary of state, William Pitt, decided to launch a new campaign against the French and their Indigenous allies in North America. He sacked the commander of British forces there, John Campbell, and replaced him with Major General James Abercrombie. Pitt wanted him to capture Fort Crown Point on the shores of Lake Champlain; Fort Louisbourg on Cape Breton Island; and Fort Duquesne.

Colonel John Forbes, commander of British forces in the southern colonies, was promoted to brigadier general, and while not directly ordered to, it was understood that he would lead the expedition against Fort Duquesne. In addition to the regular forces he already commanded, he directed the colonies to raise militias. The colonists would finance uniforms and soldiers' wages, while the Crown would pay for arms, artillery, tents and food. Virginia already had in place a regiment consisting of one thousand men under the command of Colonel Washington. Colonel William Byrd raised a second regiment of colonial soldiers. Both were put under the command of Forbes, who assembled his full army at Fort Cumberland.

Forbes asked George Washington what he could expect in the wilderness ahead and how to best tackle it. Unlike Braddock, he implemented most of Washington's suggestions. Forbes's army marched on October 26, his departure date having been delayed for want of supplies. In a letter dated August 28, he complained that the locals weren't fulfilling their contracts, leaving him without the horses and carriages he needed.

Like Braddock, Forbes found it necessary to send a smaller detachment ahead of the main force. Camped about ten miles from its goal, on November 24 its scouts reported seeing thick smoke. The next day, the British discovered that the French had mined and burned Fort Duquesne and the houses surrounding it. About thirty chimneys still stood. The British salvaged what they could, including about thirty barrels of gunpowder, and built Fort Pitt near the ruins.

While it sounds plausible that a train of mules departed containing all the fort's gold and silver that day and that the British chased after it, that would mean that such wealth existed in the first place. A traveler visiting Canada in 1749 reported seeing just a few copper French sols with a smattering of silver coins during his time there. Bartering was the most common means of exchange. High-value coins were rare despite the fact that the French crown regularly sent gold louis and silver ècus to the colony to pay its troops.

So where did it all go? Much of it was hoarded. Some was melted down for other uses. In 1704, for example, the governor of Plaisance, Jacques-François de Mombeton de Brouillan, had silver coins melted to make his dinnerware and gold coins made into jewelry—this despite the fact that doing so was illegal. Silversmiths used silver coins for their own trade. The Canadian government had a habit of devaluing its coins, another incentive for colonists to melt them down to ensure they retained their full value. The colonial government regularly issued playing cards worth various French monetary denominations, and these were by far the widest and most used currency available.

It's doubtful the entire French colonial army in Canada possessed an amount of gold and silver requiring sixteen mules to transport it. Certainly there was no reason to send that much wealth to Fort Duquesne of all places. It was in the middle of a wilderness surrounded by a mixture of hostile and allied Native people who had little use for coins. They wanted guns, gunpowder, iron and other items of practical use that they couldn't make themselves.

CHAPTER 4

JOHN DILLINGER'S LOOT

A long Route 65 about four miles outside of the village of Leipsic once stood the Pierpont family farm, where John Herbert Dillinger and members of his gang supposedly buried some of their ill-gotten gains. In 1988, *Chicago Tribune* reporter Robin Yocum interviewed Walter Schroeder, the man who owned the property at the time, and he said that treasure hunters stopped by from time to time and that he allowed them to look around but not dig. The original Pierpont house had long ago been moved elsewhere, and then it burned down. The barns used by the Pierpont family were also no more. Schroeder never bothered looking for Dillinger's loot himself. He figured if it really were buried on his property, someone would have known of its location and recovered it long ago.

During Dillinger's short bank-robbing career, which lasted from September 1933 to July 1934, he spent a surprising amount of time in Ohio. He was born into a Quaker family in Indianapolis, Indiana, on June 22, 1903, and nothing about his upbringing indicated he would become a professional criminal. His mother died when he was three, leaving his seventeen-year-old sister to serve as a surrogate. At school he liked to read, disliked math and had his share of schoolyard fights. In 1920, his father remarried and located the family to Mooresville, an Indianapolis suburb. Dillinger quit school and went to work at a machine shop and furniture factory.

He joined the navy in 1923. Punished for being absent without leave, he deserted and was dishonorably discharged. The next year, he married Beryl Hovious and went to work at an upholsterer in Mooresville. One night he got drunk and with a friend was caught trying to rob a grocery store. Convicted, he received a sentence of ten to twenty years. Sent to the state prison in Pendleton, Indiana, to serve it, his sentence was increased as punishment for a failed escape attempt. His wife divorced him in 1929.

At Pendleton, he befriended Harry Pierpont, a man considered by prison authorities to be extremely dangerous. Pierpont stood just over six feet tall and had a notable set of blue eyes. Before launching a career in crime, he had worked as an auto mechanic specializing in hydraulic hoisting. Born in 1902 in Muncie, Indiana, he was arrested for his first crime at the age of nineteen. Caught while trying to steal a car by its owner, he fired four shots at

John Dillinger. FBI. *Wikimedia Commons.*

the man that fortunately didn't cause life-threatening wounds. For this, Pierpont was sent to prison.

His mother, Lena, insisted her son's action was a prank. Writing letters and visiting the prison frequently, she made such a nuisance of herself that her son was paroled on March 6, 1923. He immediately went on a crime spree and, when caught, was sent back to Pendleton. His multiple attempts to escape resulted in solitary confinement and a transfer to Indiana State Prison North in Michigan City. Dillinger, too, was transferred there. It's here where the core of Dillinger's gang was assembled. It consisted of Dillinger, Pierpont—the brains of the operation—Homer Van Meter, John "Red" Hamilton, Charles Makley and Russell Clark.

Indiana State Prison North was built between 1860 and 1866. Its plumbing originally consisted of wooden pipes, which had to be replaced by metal ones. To pay for the prison's construction, twenty-five-cent tours were offered. Repeated prison escapes resulted in cell windows being removed and the raising of the outer wall's height. During Dillinger's time here, no guard towers existed. Those were erected in 1936.

On March 22, 1933, Dillinger was paroled. He headed home to Mooresville, where he attended a Quaker meeting during which he recanted his evil ways and pledged to live a law-abiding life. This was an act. He'd already agreed to help his friends escape from the Michigan City prison by smuggling guns to them that he would have to buy. This being the Great Depression, he figured the easiest way to raise the money for them was robbing banks.

Being a novice, his first few attempts at bank robbery yielded little. He hit it big with the robbery of the New Carlisle National Bank in Ohio, where he and his partners snagged $10,000. Instead of barging in, they hid inside overnight. On the morning of June 10, they bound two employees and forced a third to open the safe. Other robberies followed, including one on August 14 at Citizens National Bank in Bluffton.

With his ill-gotten gains, Dillinger acquired the needed guns. On September 4, he threw three of them over the wall into the yard of Indiana State Prison North. Before Pierpont and his confederates could reach them, a prisoner not part of their plot found and turned them in. Dillinger smuggled a new lot in by hiding them in a box of material sent to the prison shirt factory.

He continued to rob banks, often with his signature move of leaping over the counter, earning him the nickname "jackrabbit." His biggest take came from Indiana State Bank on Massachusetts Avenue in Indianapolis, from which $24,000 was stolen on July 17. During the Depression, most people distrusted if not outright hated banks, so for them Dillinger became a folk hero. While he wasn't known to wantonly kill or use violence, he didn't hesitate to shoot at others with the intent to kill if he felt his own life or liberty was in peril.

In late September, he went to Dayton to visit his girlfriend, Mary Longnecker. The landlady at the boardinghouse at which he stayed reported his presence to police, leading to his arrest on the twenty-second. On him, police found $2,604, five revolvers and a lot of ammunition.

On September 26, four days after Dillinger's arrest, the planned escape at Indiana State Prison North was executed. A trusty told Assistant Warden Albert Evans that he was needed in the shirt factory. There, several prisoners pointed guns at him, taking him and the shop superintendent, D.H. Stevens, hostages. Ten men escaped: Pierpont, Hamilton, Makley, Clark, John Burns, Joseph Jenkins, Edward Shouse, Walter Deitrich, Joseph Fox and James Clark. Hiding their pistols in bundles of shirts, they made their way through a series of gates. One guard, Fred Wellnitz, was too slow for them, so they slugged him on the head with a pistol barrel.

Past the main gate, they entered the prison office, where they ordered half a dozen clerks plus Evans and Stevens to enter a vault. Changing their minds, they went looking for money. One of the clerks, seventy-two-year-old Finley C. Carson, found the abrupt change in plan confusing and, for his lack of ready compliance, was shot in the leg and abdomen. The shock of his wounds caused him to fall to the floor. He fractured his skull against a table as he collapsed.

Outside, the escapees came across Sheriff Charles Neel from Corydon, Indiana, who had just dropped off two prisoners. Five of the fugitives piled into his touring car, taking him along with them. Another fugitive headed away on foot. The remaining four crossed the road to a filling station, where they told the attendant, Joe Pawlawski, to give them the keys to his car. He took to his heels. Shot at three times, one bullet grazed his shoulder and another his forehead, but neither wound impeded his escape.

Just then, Hebert Vokenburg, a tourist from Oswego, Indiana, drove by. The convicts forced his wife and mother-in-law out of the car, got in and told Vokenburg to drive. They headed toward Gary, Indiana, and after a time threw Vokenburg out. They stopped at the farm of Valley Warner near Wanatah, Indiana, where the farmer and a mail carrier were held against their will until dark, at which time they released their hostages and headed south.

Those who had kidnapped and stolen Sheriff Neel's car took his revolver. He drove them toward Chicago and then turned south onto a side road. At some point, the car crashed, forcing the escapees and their hostage to make their way on foot. They stopped at the farmhouse of Carl Spanier and forced him to drive them away in his car. He escaped while getting gas. About ten miles southwest of Michigan City, the car broke down near the farm of Carl Gustafson.

In the dark under pouring rain, they took to their feet and became hopelessly lost. For several days, they tried and failed to find Gary. Finding a car on a farm, they stole it. They also released Neel. Clark decided to travel with the sheriff, not as a captor but as an equal. On foot the two made their way to an interurban train that took them into Gary. Neel paid for Clark's ticket and bought him some food. They parted as friends, with Neel giving Clark his overcoat. Clark headed for Hammond, Indiana. Neel went to the nearest police station.

The men who rode in Vokenburg's car were Hamilton, Pierpont, Makley and Shouse. After separating from Neel, Clark joined up with them, as did another confederate who had aided the escape from the outside, Harry Copeland. The six men headed for Ohio, stopping in Makley's hometown, St. Marys, where they robbed its First National Bank to obtain money for the purchase of guns. Makley knew the bank's conservator, W.O. Smith, although he had no part in the robbery. This job yielded $11,000. Because the bills taken were so new, the fugitives had one of their girlfriends, Mary

Sheriff Jess Sarber's cap. Allen County Museum, Lima, Ohio. *Photo by the author.*

Kinder, repeatedly wash and iron them until they looked well used.

The next day, Lewis Klass, who was around nine years old, slipped onto the Pierpont Farm with his friends to look for pigeons in one of the barns. There they saw something covered with a tarp. Looking under it, they found it was a car. Just then, Mrs. Pierpont caught them. Swearing in multiple languages, she told the children to leave and never come back. Klass had no idea that the car had been used in the St. Marys robbery.

After his arrest in Dayton, Dillinger confessed to robbing the bank in Bluffton. For this, Allen County wanted to prosecute him, so it was decided to turn him over to the sheriff, Jess Sarber. When Dayton police met Sarber in Piqua, they couldn't believe he'd come without a posse of well-armed men. Didn't he realize the convicts who had escaped from Michigan City might try to break Dillinger out? Dayton police refused to release their prisoner until Sarber secured more men with guns. He took Dillinger to the Allen County Jail in Lima.

At around six o'clock in the evening on October 12, 1933, Clark, Pierpont and Makley entered Sarber's office proclaiming they were from Indiana State Prison and had come for Dillinger. Outside were Copeland, Shouse and Hamilton. Sarber asked for identification. Pierpont pulled out a revolver and proclaimed that gave him the authority he needed. Sarber supposedly went for his own pistol, which by some accounts was in a desk drawer. Pierpont responded by shooting at Sarber twice, one of the bullets hitting him in the abdomen. Pierpont and Makley pistol-whipped Sarber when he tried to get up.

Also in the room were Mrs. Sarber and Deputy Wilbur Sharp, the latter taking a nap. Sharp was ordered to give the criminals keys to the jail cells. They freed Dillinger and locked Mrs. Sarber and the deputy in a cell. The sheriff remained on his office floor bleeding out. He died two hours later. Before departing, the fugitives took two guns from the sheriff's desk: a Colt .38 Police Special with nickel plating and a Colt Detective Special with blued steel. One gun belonged to the sheriff, the other to the deputy. The seven men drove away in a Chrysler sedan and an Essex coach and briefly stopped at the Pierpont Farm.

Deputy Wilbur Sharp's revolver was taken by Dillinger's gang during the jail breakout. Allen County Museum, Lima, Ohio. *Photo by the author.*

Shortly after the breakout, Lima's chief of police, J.W. Cook, interviewed Mrs. Sarber. She identified Pierpont from a photo as the shooter, so the chief gathered a posse and headed north to his family's farm. They arrived at around ten o'clock that night but found no trace of the bandits. In the barn, they discovered an Oldsmobile without any license plates—the one Klass had seen.

The next day, the Putman County sheriff, Wilson Crafis, arrested Harry Pierpont's brother Fred for possession of the Olds because it was the getaway car used for the St. Marys bank robbery. It belonged to Arthur S. Cherrington of Chicago—an alias used by Copeland. On the night of that heist, the bandits had stopped at the Pierpont Farm. There, Harry told Fred there was a car in Hamilton at a certain address, and he could have if he went to get it. The next day, Fred's parents and grandmother drove him to pick up the vehicle.

From this point on, the Dillinger Gang did all its robbing in Indiana, Illinois and Wisconsin. Just two days after the breakout in Lima, three of its members broke into the police station in Auburn, Indiana, and stole a number of guns and three bulletproof vests. A week later, they hit another police station in Peru, Indiana. From both they took pistols, rifles and Thompson submachine guns.

After another string of bank robberies in Indiana, they headed to Chicago to spend their ill-gotten gains. Dividing their take, they spent it on a wide variety of things, some of it being mundane such as getting dental work done. They bought expensive gifts for their girlfriends and nice clothes for themselves. They went to restaurants, bars, ballgames and, in Dillinger's case, the movie theater. He also paid for a divorce for his Dayton girlfriend, Mary. He frequented whorehouses in part because they served as meeting places for the underworld.

On November 20, 1933, the gang robbed the American Bank & Trust Company bank in Racine, Wisconsin, a job they pulled off with Tommy guns, with which they wounded two men. Kidnapping three others, they made off with about $28,000 in money and securities. Dollars were easy to spend, but the securities they stole were more difficult to cash in. Two years after Dillinger's 1934 death, a New York City policeman arrested a fence named Albert Montlake in the Bowery. His cache of stolen goods worth $13,000 was found at the midtown hotel where he lived. It included $10,000 worth of the securities taken by the Dillinger Gang.

The City of Chicago set up a "Dillinger Squad" consisting of forty men, but all they did was kill three men they mistook as members of his gang. By that time, most of its real members, Dillinger among them, had headed to Florida for the Christmas holiday. After this, Dillinger, Makley and Pierpont went to Arizona. A tipoff led local police to find and arrest them. Dillinger was extradited to Indiana and incarcerated in the Crown Point County Jail, from which he escaped on March 3, 1934, using a wooden gun darkened with black shoe polish. He immediately returned to robbing banks, forming a new gang that included Lester Joseph Gillis, better known as Baby Face Nelson.

Pierpont, Clark and Makley were extradited to Lima to stand trial for the murder of Sheriff Sarber. Dillinger wanted to free his friends but realized it would be suicide because National Guardsmen manning machine gun nests protected the county courthouse. A jury found the three men on trial guilty of murder. Pierpont and Makley received death sentences. Clark got life. They were taken to the Ohio State Penitentiary in Columbus for safekeeping.

Pierpont's mother, Lena, insisted her son was innocent and that he never lied. She claimed that Van Meter shot the sheriff, but he wasn't even there. Harry's father was in the same mind as his wife. He insisted all the stories about his son were lies. Lena denied knowing Dillinger, but that certainly wasn't true. He visited her on March 23, 1934, and was upset that she had received only half of the $1,000 he'd sent her via his lawyer. He gave her the other $500 on the spot. He visited the Pierpont Farm one more time between April 5 and 8. If any loot really was buried there, he had plenty of chances to retrieve it.

Harry and Makley had no intention of allowing the State of Ohio to execute them. When a guard brought Pierpont lunch, he overpowered and beat this man. Grabbing his keys, he freed Makley and Clark. Taking inspiration from Dillinger, they produced guns carved out of soap and then freed all but one prisoner in L block. They used the fake guns to convince two guards to release them. As they fled, they were gunned down by a squad of guards. Makley was killed outright and Pierpont hit in the spine, paralyzing him. The State of Ohio executed him on October 17, 1934. He barely ate his last meal of chicken. He said nothing before being put to death via the electric chair. A death mask was placed on his face.

Dillinger remained free until the day of his death, which preceded Pierpont's. On the evening of July 24, 1934, Dillinger went to Biograph Theater in Chicago to see *Manhattan Melodrama*. Accompanying him were Etta Natalsky and Theresa Paulus. At 10:40 that night, the three exited the theater into an alley where sixteen Bureau of Investigation agents waited for him. They opened fire and killed their target in short order. Whether Dillinger reached for a gun is debatable.

The two women suffered no serious injuries. At this point, Dillinger had had plastic surgery, but the man in charge of the agents, Melvin Purvis, said he recognized Dillinger right away. He had, after all, stared at photos of him long enough. The agents knew Dillinger was there because of intelligence provided by Romanian brothel owner Ana Sage, who'd given him up in exchange for $25,000 and a promise she'd be helped to avoid deportation. The Department of Labor sent her back to Romania in 1936.

CHAPTER 5

MILES OGLE'S BURIED COUNTERFEIT MONEY

Over his long career as a professional counterfeiter, it's said that Miles Ogle buried all sorts of items related to his profession, including plates for printing counterfeit money, fake bills and good money. Most of the stories are problematic. One says when he was about to be apprehended by authorities, he covered a set of counterfeit plates in paraffin wax, wrapped them in silk, covered that with more paraffin wax, wrapped this in rubber, put them in a crock, covered that in paraffin and wrapped this in oilcloth. He buried the package in a vacant lot near Camp Washington's Colerain Avenue bridge. But there was no bridge on that street. A city map from 1900, the year Ogle died, shows the closest one was one to the southeast that connected Clearwater and Stark Streets across the since-removed Miami and Erie Canal.

Ogle also buried cash and plates around the Cincinnati neighborhood of Brighton. More was buried along present-day Baltimore Avenue in the Cincinnati neighborhood of South Fairmount. But the granddaddy of all Ogle tales appeared in the *Cincinnati Enquirer*. It reported that after dying in his cell at the Ohio State Penitentiary in Columbus, he left behind a map of part of Kentucky with coded language pointing to where he'd hidden his wealth. But by that point in his life, he'd been incapacitated by a stroke. He also died in a hospital room, not his prison cell.

In nineteenth-century America, counterfeiting was rampant and big business. Counterfeiters were known as "coneymen." Their fake bills and coins were known as "queer." Those who made counterfeit money rarely

Right: Miles Ogle, 1885. *Library of Congress.*

Below: Map of Cincinnati, by Eugene Murray-Aaron and George Franklin Cram, 1901. *Dave Rumsey Map Collection.*

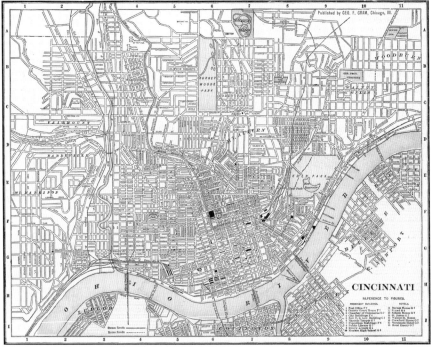

distributed it themselves. Instead, they sold it at a discount to shovers or passers, who "spread the queer" in order to get real money in return. Before the introduction of federally issued money in 1862, banks issued their own currency, making catching coneymen even harder. During the Civil War, it is estimated that about one-third of all money circulating in the United States was fake. To counter this, Congress created the Secret Service. President Lincoln signed the bill creating this agency hours before his assassination.

Ogle was a master engraver whose work was especially difficult to detect. Of German parentage, he was born in 1841 in the state of New York. His family left while he was still young and spent several years roaming around eastern Ohio and western Pennsylvania. In 1862, Ogle; his father, George; his brother John; and his mother bought a flatboat. From a point near Cincinnati, they headed down the Ohio River toward the Mississippi, robbing and plundering along the way. Although they were detained at Louisville, Kentucky, authorities released them for want of evidence. While they were at Rockport, Indiana, a law officer boarded their boat. Ogle shot the fellow in the breast, killing him. For this, he was sentenced to five years prison in Jefferson, Indiana.

This was an unpleasant place to be sent. Known as Indiana State Prison South, the northern one being in Michigan City (where Dillinger would later be incarcerated—see chapter 4), it was built in 1821 to replace whipping posts. Prison labor constructed this edifice, which covered sixteen acres. Unventilated cell blocks were no more than dungeons through which disease ran rampant. Prisoners manufactured things. During Ogle's time here, they made farm implements and wagons.

Upon serving his full sentence, Ogle joined the notorious Reno Gang. The paternal grandfather of this brood, James Reno, moved in 1813 from Kentucky to Indiana's Jackson County, where he started a farm near Rockwell. One of his sons, Frank, married and produced at least one daughter and five boys: Frank, James, Simeon, Clinton and William. Frank instilled in them a strict interpretation of religion. The older boys disliked both that and school.

In 1863, Congress implemented a military draft that had a provision allowing a conscripted person to pay $300 to get out of service or to find a substitute. Frank and James gamed this system by agreeing to become substitutes, taking the bonus money they were paid for signing up and then deserting. They also acted as brokers to find substitutes for others. They returned to the family farm in 1864, bringing with them some of their unsavory associates who became members of their new gang. Brothers

Simeon (Sim) and William also joined. Clinton and their sister Laura declined to do so.

The Reno Gang made its unofficial headquarters at the Rader House hotel in the Jackson County town of Seymour, Indiana. Here guest rooms were frequently robbed, and in 1866, a guest was found beheaded and floating in the nearby White River. The gang robbed, murdered and terrorized the region. On October 6, 1866, it robbed an Ohio and Mississippi Railroad train leaving Seymour. This is possibly the first peacetime train robbery in U.S. history. A passenger, George Kinney, recognized the robbers, who included John and Sim Reno as well as Frank Sparks, who were arrested but released on bail. Kinney was murdered at his home shortly after, causing the case against the Renos to collapse.

John, the brains of the operation, was recognized during the robbery of the treasurer's office at Davies County Courthouse in Missouri. Arrested, he pleaded guilty on January 18, 1868, and received a sentence of twenty-five years in prison. Frank took over the gang. Ogle joined and participated in a series of robberies in Iowa and one of a train in Marshfield, Indiana. From this, the gang stole about $96,000 in cash, government bonds and currency notes. Afterward, Frank, Ogle and several other gang members went to Windsor, Ontario, to evade pursing authorities.

Outraged by the Reno Gang's activities, citizens of Jackson County formed a vigilance committee sometimes known as the Scarlet Mask Society on account of the fact that they wore long red bandanas when going about their extrajudicial business. Authorities repeatedly caught members of the Reno Gang only to have them snatched by the Scarlet Mask Society, which usually hanged its prisoners. The last gang members to be apprehended by law enforcement were taken to a stone jail in Indiana's Floyd County, a place Sheriff Thomas J. Fullenlove considered impenetrable. He was wrong. On the night of December 11, 1868, about one hundred of the vigilantes stormed it and hanged the gang members within.

Ogle had parted ways with the gang before this incident, making his way to Fort Wayne, Indiana, where he learned the art of counterfeiting from John Peter McCartney. Born in Illinois, McCartney had little education and was semiliterate. While working in Mattoon, Illinois, he met a family of counterfeiters, the Johnsons, from whom he learned engraving. One of the Johnson women, Ida, married Miles Ogle, and undoubtedly this is how he became acquainted with McCartney.

McCartney perfected the art of engraving under the tutelage of Ben Boyd. McCartney pioneered the idea of scraping off the values of one-dollar bills

"Engraving Plates for Printing Money, Bureau of Printing and Engraving, Washington, D.C." Keystone View Company, June 22, 1917. *Library of Congress.*

and changing them to five or ten. He would pass these in Indianapolis, the city where he lived when not incarcerated. Imprisonment was usually brief: he was a master of escaping. He abandoned the scraping scheme in favor of bleaching low-denomination bills and printing higher-valued denominations on this genuine paper. He also developed a machine to mimic the scrollwork on treasury notes. Between 1866 and 1868, he traveled throughout the West in the guise of Professor Joseph Woods giving lectures on how to detect counterfeit money.

In 1868, Ogle and partner James Lyons printed twenty-dollar treasury notes in Fort Wayne using McCartney's plates and then moved their operation to Rolla, Missouri, for the next two years. At some point, Ogle stole from McCartney $75,000 worth of counterfeit $5 bills that he sold to shovers in Cincinnati. Arrested in Philadelphia, Pennsylvania, on March 12, 1873, Ogle was taken to Pittsburgh, Pennsylvania, from which he'd jumped bail for an earlier arrest. He surrendered the copper plates for $5 U.S. treasury notes and steel plates for fifty-cent notes issued as U.S. fractional currency—paper money representing less than one dollar. He also turned over a considerable number of counterfeit bills.

He convinced the U.S. district attorney for the Western District of Pennsylvania, Henry Bucher Swope, that he was going straight and promised to use his intimate knowledge of the counterfeiting business to wipe it out in the United States forever. After giving up a few fellow counterfeiters, he was released on bail on October 18. Skipping, he moved to the Cincinnati suburb

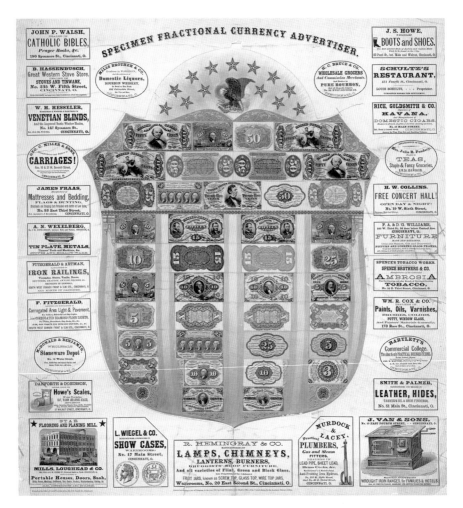

Specimen Fractional Currency Advertiser. John Tanner & Co., circa 1867. *Library of Congress.*

Chevoit, where, according to John S. Dye's 1880 *Government Blue Book*, "he rented a small farm and kept a country variety store." This he abandoned when authorities came too close for comfort.

He remained at liberty for several years, still engraving plates to print fake bills. In 1875, Secret Service agents Estes C. Rathbone and F.C. Tuttle were assigned to Cincinnati. Keen on catching Ogle, they learned that he'd been seen at a tavern owned by John McKernan at 84 Front Street. Armed with a description of Ogle—he was a stout man of about six feet in height with semi-curly brown hair whose good looks would one day be ruined by too much drinking—Estes and Tuttle watched the tavern for about a month. Ogle made an appearance on the night of January 6, 1876. The detectives later learned that their suspect printed his counterfeit bills here.

They followed him to a livery on the east side of Freeman Street that he owned under the alias J.F. Oglesby. Next he went to his house at 243 Poplar Street, at which he met his brother-in-law William Rhodes Johnson. Estes and Tuttle followed the two to a train station, where the agents disguised themselves as brakemen by soiling their faces and hands with dirt. Ogle and Johnson bought tickets for an eastbound train, got on and sat apart from each other as if they didn't know each other. After cleaning themselves up, the detectives boarded as well.

Ogle and Johnson detrained at Brighton, a place where coneymen were known to meet. Checking regularly to make sure they weren't followed, they made their way to a certain elm tree where they "raised a plant"—that is, dug up a valise. At that moment, the detectives made their arrest, subduing Ogle before he could grab his revolver. In the valise was $5,000 in counterfeit bills and plates for printing $10 bills for about forty national banks in Indiana. Taken to Pittsburgh for trial, Ogle was convicted and sent to prison, where he spent the next eight years.

When he got out in July 1883, Ogle decided to revenge himself upon society by engraving new plates for a twenty-dollar silver certificate and another set for ten-dollar ones for the Third National Bank of Cincinnati. He procured a flatboat near Parkersburg, West Virginia, on which he put the tools of his trade. Partnered with his brother John, he headed down the Ohio River, selling counterfeit bills to shovers all along the route. He eluded authorities in city after city.

Captain M.G. Bauer of the Secret Service saw Ogle in Cincinnati but didn't arrest him for lack of hard evidence. Guessing Ogle was headed south, Bauer boarded a train headed to Memphis, Tennessee. Coupled to Bauer's train was a sleeper car that had been detached from a train traveling between the Tennessee cities of Evansville and Nashville. Bauer found Ogle sleeping in this car. At Memphis, Bauer shadowed Ogle with the help of Chief of Police Davis and Detective Pryde. They apprehended Ogle outside St. Mary's Catholic Church on Christmas Day. One newspaper account says he surrendered without a fight. Another says that there was an intense struggle. On him they found $3,000 in fake Third National Bank $10 bills and $610 in good money.

In mid-January, another $20,000 of $10 counterfeit bills was found hidden in Kentucky. At the Union Stockyards, which were about three miles outside Cincinnati, authorities dug up another $35,000 in fake bills plus the tools, plates and paper used to print them. Also found were fake $20 silver certificates. For this crime, Ogle spent six years at a federal prison in Chester, Illinois. Upon getting out in 1890, he claimed to have gone straight. He spent time in Cincinnati and St. Louis, Missouri.

In 1890, ten-dollar Germania National Bank of New Orleans, Louisiana counterfeit bills began circulating at a Louisville racetrack. These were so good that the *San Francisco Call* called them "dangerous." One of the shovers, John Smith, was arrested and sentenced to eight years at Kentucky's Frankfort Penitentiary. The other shovers escaped. Bauer and another agent, Donnella, began looking for Ogle. In Newport, Kentucky, they found a white-whiskered man dressed in a long black coat who resembled a clergyman. The detectives weren't fooled. This was Ogle.

They arrested him during his crossing of a bridge over the Licking River to Covington, Kentucky. He struggled but was overpowered. On his person, the detectives found $2,000 in good money but nothing incriminating. Given a bond of $15,000, he was sent to jail. Ogle swore he was innocent and hadn't made the Germania plates. He'd been framed. After being held for three months, he was sent to Memphis. The plates were never recovered, so Ogle was charged with selling counterfeit money. Found guilty, he was given fifteen years in the Ohio Penitentiary in Columbus.

In his last years, he suffered from paralysis, leaving him unable to move

William J. Burns. Photo by Arnold Genthe, circa May 18 or July 6, 1907. *Library of Congress.*

his legs or speak. Hillsboro's *News-Herald* reported that Ogle was "a helpless invalid." He died on June 27, 1900, at Mount Carmel Hospital in Columbus. The Germania counterfeits outlived him. In August 1905, one of his fake ten-dollar bills showed up in Missouri.

His death prompted Secret Service agent William J. Burns to look for the Germania plates. Burns, who later opened a famous detective agency with ethical problems, didn't find them. They may well be buried somewhere. This is one of the few instances where buried treasure shows up in the historical record in a verifiable way. But even if a person did find the plates, or a cache of Ogle's fake money, it wouldn't make them rich. So far as this author knows, there's no market for counterfeit plates made for obsolete money that no one could spend anyway. It is possible Ogle buried good money, but criminals such as he tended to spend it as quickly as they got it, making this highly unlikely.

Chapter 6

ANDREW MEYER'S HOARD

That Andrew Meyer was rich when he arrived in Baltimore, Maryland, there can be no doubt. It's the source of the wealth that's debatable. One story says he fought side by side with Napoléon and brought with him to America a jewel-encrusted chest filled with loot gained while on campaign. Another tale claims it was his uncle (or possibly brother) Francis who brought it over. Francis was a colonel in the French army who'd fought for France in Russia and at Waterloo.

For the latter, he was said to have received the Legion of Honor and a fancy sword, but this is patently false. French veterans of Waterloo weren't given commendations until 1857, at which time those still living received the St. Helena medal created by Emperor Napoléon III. Francis supposedly brought to America an iron box used to carry the payroll for the French army on campaigns that presumably contained great wealth. A newspaper report from 1924 in the *Canton Daily News* reported the box was still on display at the Meyer mansion.

A third story has Meyer burying money on the grounds of his mansion or claims that he sank a boat carrying a copper kettle filled with gold into the lake named after him. These tales have attracted treasure hunters, people who employed divining rods, hypnotists and clairvoyants without any success. In 1924, boys who'd heard that gold was plowed up on Meyer's land every so often searched along the shore of Meyers Lake. They, like everyone else, found nothing. Andrew Meyer's descendants thought little of these stories. It was well known he'd invested much of his wealth in real estate.

The historical record, such as it is, leaves much to desire when it comes to details such as Meyer's birthplace. One source says he was born in Bonn, then part of Prussia, and another in Alsace, France. Prussia is the more likely spot. His year of birth, too, isn't set in stone. It's either 1761 or 1762. Well educated and with some royal blood in his veins, for much of his life he was a professional solider, serving in the Austrian army against the Turks in a war between them that lasted from 1788 and 1791. For a time, he was an officer in the French army, but he ultimately fought against Napoléon for nine years.

The year when Meyer immigrated to the United States isn't fixed, either. Some sources say 1791, others 1802. They all agree that he settled in Baltimore. Here he, his brother Godfrey and other partners started a business that molded and burnished brass for the U.S. government. In 1803, Andrew married the widow of one of his now-deceased partners, Cordelia Gross Haasafratz, with whom he had five children.

He was also the sole owner of two ships and part owner of others. When the War of 1812 broke out, he converted at least one of his vessels and possibly more into a privateer to harass British cargo ships. One source says he operated two privateers, the *Joseph* and *Mary*, but a list of active privateers during that war only has a single ship out of Baltimore named the *Joseph and Mary* commanded by Captain William Wescott.

The *General Armstrong* commanded by Captain Sam C. Reid is an example of what an American privateer ship from the War of 1812 looked like, circa 1838 to 1856. *Library of Congress.*

On November 25, 1812, Westcott watched the *Nonsuch* detain the schooner *Mary*. He sailed to the *Mary*'s rescue, and a spirited battle erupted between his ship and the *Nonsuch* during which two men died and four others were wounded. *Joseph and Mary* was overtaken by men on the *Nonsuch*'s boats and forced to surrender. To his embarrassment, it was then that Captain Wescott learned the *Nonsuch* was an American privateer that had stopped the *Mary* because she was suspected of shipping cargo for the British. Wescott apologized.

Meyer fought for his adopted country at the Maryland battles of Baltimore—the inspiration for Francis Scott Key's "Star-Spangled Banner"—and Bladensburg, the loss of which allowed the British to march unopposed into Washington, D.C., part of which they burned. After Bladensburg, a general gave Meyer a fine rifle to thank him for standing his ground, a treasure he valued all his life.

To compensate him for the loss of at least one of his privateers, the U.S. government gifted Meyer a considerable number of acres of wilderness in what is now Stark County. He and his brother-in-law Joseph Shorb traveled there in 1816 and built a small house. Meyer returned home for his wife and children. The family headed to Ohio under armed guard to protect them from criminals and hostile Native Americans. Mrs. Meyer brought with her a beautiful rare clock she kept on her lap the entire trip. The family settled in a place by a lake then known as the Great Spring, now called Meyers Lake. They were probably the first Roman Catholics to settle in what would one day become the Canton area.

Meyer purchased additional land abutting his from Canton's founder, Bazaleel Wells, for eleven dollars an acre, increasing the total amount he owned to nearly three thousand acres. He founded Sweet Spring Farm, on which he raised Merino sheep and grew wheat. He opened a dry goods store in Canton and had a mansion built. At first, bricks for it were imported from Zanesville, but transport was difficult, so a brickwork was built on the site. Wood was imported from Baltimore and the flooring from Steubenville. On the mansion's door was a brass knocker that read, "Andrew Meyer, Sr., 1822," the year of the house's completion. It had twelve rooms and three floors, the upper ones being accessible by a grand staircase.

Meyer died at the age of eighty-six. His wealth went to his heirs. Several generations of his descendants occupied the mansion until the early 1970s. At that point, its last resident, Helen Meyer Follen, could no longer maintain the decaying place. She tried to sell it to Stark County

Historical Society for $500,000, but they weren't interested, not even after she lowered the price to $100,000. After her departure, looters stole nearly all its interior fixtures. It burned down on October 28, 1975. The area where the mansion was built has since been built over, leaving the only places to look for "lost" treasure northeast of the Lehman Middle School or in and around Meyers Lake.

CHAPTER 7

LOOT FROM MORGAN'S RAID

The Union troops being ferried on the Muskingham River by the gunboat *Dime* disembarked at Rokeby. Under the command of R.W. McFarland, they were part of the Eighty-Sixth Regiment from Zanesville and on the hunt for Brigadier General John Hunt Morgan and his Confederate raiders. While on top of Barr's Ridge on the Eli Barr Farm, McFarland saw the Rebels in a hollow below. His men fired at long range, and McFarland later recalled he didn't think they'd hit anyone.

A dead Confederate soldier with a pillow placed under his head was found here by a couple of civilians. The next day, he was buried. His grave was marked with a sandstone tablet that said, "Tommy McGee." Twenty years later, a rumor emerged that some of McGee's comrades had returned in search for loot they left behind near where his body was left. It's believed that McGee was killed at nearby Eagleport and that the attack by McFarland enticed the Rebels to abandon his body in the narrow hollow.

The night before his capture, Morgan is said to have had $5,000 worth of gold buried that he'd extorted from mill owners in Indiana (more on that later). In 1905, a Confederate veteran who said he'd been one of Morgan's raiders appeared on the Hansaker Farm in Hocking County. He claimed a detachment of men trying to shake Union pursuers around Nelsonville buried an iron pot filled with gold, jewels and other valuables. The veteran went looking for this around Berry Hollows and Oil Well but found nothing.

Morgan's raid caused many Ohioans to panic. The owner of a farm about a mile south of McArthur in Vinton County, Tom Felton, thought it

General John Morgan,
circa 1870–90. *Library of
Congress.*

best to protect his wealth by burying an iron pot that contained about $200 worth of gold coins plus his wife's silverware. After the danger passed, he couldn't remember where he'd buried it and never did find it. While stories of Ohioans burying their wealth are true, this particular one is a bit dubious. Morgan's raid lasted just a couple of weeks, and surely Felton couldn't have had that bad of a memory.

Morgan's primary goal in invading Ohio wasn't to plunder but rather to disrupt Union plans for the summer of 1863. At this time, the Confederacy was feeling the Union's bite in the western theater. Confederate general Simon Bolivar Buckner didn't have enough men to effectively defend against Union assaults in eastern Tennessee, and his commanding officer, General Braxton Bragg, couldn't spare men to reinforce him because of the pressure put on him by Union general William S. Rosecrans. Union general Ambrose Burnside, headquartered in Cincinnati and in overall command in the Department of Ohio, was preparing to send troops to reinforce Rosecrans in Tennessee.

Bragg planned to move his force from around Tullahoma, Tennessee, across the Tennessee River and make his stand near Chattanooga, Tennessee, but he needed breathing room, so he ordered Morgan to launch a cavalry raid into Kentucky to tie up Union troops. Morgan wanted to invade Indiana and Ohio, but Bragg forbade him from doing so.

Morgan wasn't a man who often followed rules. He was once suspended from Kentucky's Transylvania University for dueling. His time in the cavalry during the Mexican-American War gave him a taste for the military, but downsizing after the peace kept him from making a career of it. He made investments in the woolen and hemp industries and also became a slave trader. Fearing for that institution's longevity because those damned Yankees seemed hell-bent on abolishing it, he joined a proslavery Kentucky militia that integrated into the Confederate army after the Civil War broke out.

Morgan's force consisted of 2,460 men armed with three Parrott guns and several howitzers. Heavy rains soaked the region for about ten days, swelling the rivers. On July 2, his force crossed the Cumberland River near Sparta, Tennessee, virtually unopposed because the Union general commanding the area, Henry M. Judah, thought the high water would prevent Morgan from crossing. He and his men headed to Columbia, Kentucky, where they attacked the town of Lebanon, Kentucky, on July 5. During this fight, Morgan's younger brother was killed, but it didn't slow the pace.

Defying orders, Morgan decided to invade Ohio. To that end, he sent two companies ahead to find boats to cross the Ohio River. They stole the *J.J. McCombs* and *Alice Dean* at Brandenburg, Kentucky. While they were ferrying troops across the river into Indiana, the Union gunboat *Springfield* appeared. It attempted to interfere, but Morgan's Parrott guns forced it to retreat.

An Indiana militia consisting of about one hundred soldiers tried to prevent the Confederates from gaining a foothold in their state, but Morgan's much larger force made short work of them, killing two. Stiffer resistance between the Indiana towns of Mauckport and Corydon delayed Morgan's force for five hours. Brigadier General Edward H. Hobson was in pursuit with his own cavalry, but even after Morgan's delay, he was still four hours behind. The Rebels went mostly unopposed while in Indiana.

One of Morgan's men, Curtis R. Burke, kept a detailed war journal. Born in Massillon, he lived in a variety of places in Ohio, including Zanesville and Mount Vernon, until moving to Kentucky at the age of nine. His father ran a marble business. The family lived in the Kentucky cities of Marysville and Frankfurt before settling permanently in Lexington. Burke's father was a sergeant in Morgan's company of Lexington Rifles, which Curtis later joined.

Left: General Henry M. Judah. Brady's National Photographic Portrait Galleries, circa 1860–66. *Library of Congress.*

Right: Brigadier General Edward Henry Hobson. Webster & Bro. Photographic Gallery, 1863. *Library of Congress.*

On July 7, Morgan's force stayed the night at a farmhouse recently abandoned by its occupants. The men helped themselves to the grain stored outside as well as "meat and bread in the house[,] then [we] got into the milk, butter and preserves in the dairy." At Salem, Indiana, they stole horses, a wagon and ammunition. In Canton, Indiana, they fed their horses at a corncrib and took what grain they could carry. Boots and shoes were stolen from a shoemaker. Burke, in desperate need of the latter, acquired a pair here. The Rebels took their ill-gotten cash and used it to purchase items they didn't outright steal, such as hard cider.

The provost marshal accompanying Morgan's men, Major Steele, tried to stop the looting, but this was an effort in futility. In his book *A History of Morgan's Calvary*, Morgan's brother-in-law and second-in-command, Basil Duke, wrote:

Calico was the staple article of appropriation—each man (who could get one) tied a bolt of it to his saddle, only to throw it away and get a fresh one at the first opportunity. They did not pillage with any sort of method or reason—it seemed to be a mania, senseless and purposeless. One man carried a bird-cage, with three canaries in it, for two days. Another rode with a chafing-dish, which looked like a small metallic coffin, on the pummel of his saddle, until an officer forced him to throw it away. Although the weather was intensely warm, another…slung seven pairs of skates around his neck, and chuckled over his acquisition. I saw very few articles of real value taken—they pillaged like boys robbing an orchard. I would not have believed that such a passion could have been developed, so ludicrously, among any body of civilized men.

As Morgan's force approached Corydon, it captured a state senator, S.K. Wolfe, and county auditor, S.W. Douglas. They were made to ride at the front of the column proclaiming if any citizen fired at the Rebels, it would mean the death of everyone in town. Morgan threatened to torch Leffler & Applegate and Wright & Brown flouring mills unless they paid him paid $500 each, which they did. There is no evidence they paid in gold; more likely it was in Union greenbacks. The raiders robbed two of the town's general stores of $5,524 in merchandise and still more from Dr. Reader's drugstore. They stole $750 from the town's treasurer.

From Indiana's Harrison County, the Rebels stole between 300 and 400 horses. This pattern they repeated throughout their raid not because they needed them—most of them were useless for military purposes, and they often went lame—but to keep them out of the hands of the Union soldiers following them. Despite this, Hobson's pursuing men managed to confiscate 150 horses from the county. It's estimated that Morgan's and Hobson's forces used up to 25,000 horses in their fast-paced crossing of Indiana and Ohio. Certainly it was a minimum of 10,000. Later, when Indiana allowed claims to be filed for compensation for what was taken, the citizens of Harrison County claimed a total of $86,552 in property lost to Rebel looting and Union confiscations.

Morgan's force crossed the border into Ohio at Harrison. From there, it rode close to Loveland, then Goshen, New Boston and Williamsburg. In Batavia, more horses were stolen. The Rebels stopped for several hours in Winchester to strip it of anything useful or valuable. Worried that he might clash with Burnside's army in Cincinnati, Morgan pushed his men hard for thirty-five hours straight, during which they rode for ninety miles. It wasn't until they reached Williamsburg that Morgan allowed them to rest.

Major General Ambrose Burnside.
Brady's National Photographic
Portrait Galleries, circa 1860–66.
Library of Congress.

At this point, he was down to fewer than two thousand men, the rest having been lost to skirmishes or left behind because they couldn't keep up. Morgan had George Ellsworth tap the telegraph lines to make himself aware of Union movements. Ellsworth was so good at this that he earned the nickname "Lightning." Sometimes Morgan had him send out fake messages to further confuse Burnside, who found trying to coordinate the search for the Confederate force by telegraph frustrating.

On July 13, Burnside declared martial law in Cincinnati as well as the Kentucky cities of Covington and Newport across the river. In Cincinnati itself, he had only 1,500 militia troops, so he called in the three regiments from Lawrence, Indiana, to bolster his defenses. He didn't have sufficient trained men stationed in Cincinnati to attack the Rebels as they passed around it.

Burnside was born in Liberty, Indiana, on May 23, 1824. He graduated from West Point Military Academy in 1847 with a ranking of eighteenth out of thirty-eight in his class. He saw no action during the Mexican-American War. "Bored," says *American National Biography*, "he gambled away six months' pay." He fought Apaches along the Santa Fe Trail, where he concluded that the U.S. Army desperately needed breech-loading rifles. With that idea in mind, he resigned in 1853 and opened a factory to manufacture carbines in Bristol, Rhode Island. A lack of military contracts resulted in its failure.

His friend George B. McClellan arranged for him to become the treasurer of the Illinois Central Railroad, which got him out of debt. At the outbreak of the Civil War, Burnside joined the Union army and briefly served as the commander of the Army of the Potomac. Although he was not a bad general, in 1865 he resigned shortly after his failure at the Battle of the Crater in Petersburg, Virginia. His prodigious beard growing on the sides of his face gave the English language the word "sideburns."

At his request, Ohio governor David Tod called up fifty thousand militiamen to deal with the invading Confederates. At Williamsburg, Morgan's force divided in two. Colonel Richard Morgan took his half southeast while Morgan led his northeast. In Piketon, a soldier stormed into a store right past the guard posted in front of it and stuffed his pockets with horn buttons. Also here and in Jasper, Morgan burned two canalboats hauling weapons. His men picked Jackson clean and burned Burn's Flour Mill, which caused an estimated $18,000 in damage. The Rebels were hampered by trees felled across the roads to slow them down.

Morgan's divided force reunited at Hanesville in Meigs County on July 18. It headed for the unincorporated community of Portland, which was just north of Buffington Island. The Rebels arrived at about eight o'clock in the evening. By this time, they had nearly exhausted their supply of ammunition. The Portland ford was guarded by about three hundred Union men and two artillery pieces behind an earthwork. Morgan decided to attack it in the morning to allow his exhausted men and horses to rest, and for a heavy fog to dissipate.

The Confederate attack overwhelmed the entrenched force. Hobson's cavalry arrived about an hour later just as Morgan's men tried to cross the five-foot-high water. Fire from Hobson's men and Union gunboats prevented most of the Rebels from getting to the West Virginian side of the river. About seven hundred Rebels were taken prisoner, one of whom was Burke. In his journal, he recorded, "We threw away nearly everything that we had got on the raid. All of the pistols were thrown as far into the bushes as we could throw them.…Some of the boys even threw away green backs [*sic*] and watches for fear that the Yanks would treat them rough if they found such things about them.…There was [*sic*] enough things scattered through the woods to set up quite a respectable variety store." The prisoners waded into the Ohio River and bathed alongside Hobson's men as if they were old friends.

General Judah showed up after the fighting ended. As the ranking officer, he took charge of both the men and the prisoners and then sent a telegraph to Burnside telling him of the Confederate defeat. This didn't please Hobson. Morgan wasn't among those captured. He and about 1,200 men escaped north. Riding for fifteen or twenty miles, they tried crossing the Ohio again. About mid-stream, Union gunboats arrived, stopping the procession. Morgan and about 900 of his men were forced back to the Ohio side of the river. They headed west. Hobson's, Judah's and General Benjamin Piatt Runkle's troops pursued. Surrounded on three sides, it appeared Morgan and his men would soon be caught. But that night, the wily general led them single file along a steep hillside that the Union commanders didn't think could be crossed. In the morning, the Rebels were nowhere to be seen. They crossed three counties, reaching Perry County on June 22.

The Rebels headed to Rokeby Lock in Morgan County (named for a Revolutionary War hero), where about twenty Union officers saw them, resulting in a brief skirmish that failed to slow their pace. Morgan aimed to cross the Muskingum River to Eagleport via a ferry, but not all his men could fit at once, so he abandoned this idea and headed north. Seeing the steamer *Dime* carrying Union troops under the command of R.W. McFarland out of Zanesville, the Rebels headed back toward Rokeby and then turned northeast. It's here where the incident outlined in the opening paragraphs of this chapter occurred.

On a Sunday morning, the Rebels rode into a small settlement about two miles south of Salineville in Columbiana County. Some of its citizens fled into the woods. Morgan and his men helped themselves to the food left behind. After this impromptu breakfast, Morgan asked a local, H.J. Boice, if he had any word about Union troops in Hammondsville to the southeast. Brice said it was filled with them. How about Salineville? The seventeen-year-old Brice said none were in that place, well knowing that Robert McMillen had just ridden there to warn the soldiers there of Morgan's arrival.

The Union troops in Salineville were a regiment from Pennsylvania that had arrived by train at one o'clock in the morning that day. The townsfolk, knowing Morgan was close, shut their houses and shops while many women and children fled carrying what worldly goods they could. When Morgan saw the regiment, he and his men turned a different direction. A skirmish erupted. Morgan, driving a carriage pulled by two white horses, abandoned this for a horse and escaped with a few of his men.

They made their way to East Liverpool, where a regiment under the command of Major George W. Rue intercepted him. Rue, a man of French descent whose family name was originally LaRue, had a public school education and was a farmer when the Mexican-American War broke out. Born in Harrodsburg, Kentucky, he enlisted as a private on May 19, 1846. After serving in that conflict, he mustered out and returned to farming in Kentucky. At the age of thirty-four, he became a major in the Ninth Kentucky Cavalry, which had been formed on August 22, 1862.

On the day Morgan's force crossed into Indiana, Rue was in Kentucky recovering from an illness. His attempt to return to his regiment in Cincinnati ran into a snag. He tried to cross the Ohio via a train, but the conductor refused him because he wore his uniform and soldiers without passes from their superiors could not board. Rue went to a friend's, changed into civilian clothes and took the next train to Cincinnati. There he reported to Burnside.

Several days later, Burnside ordered him to take one thousand men from the Covington Barracks along with horses to pursue Morgan. Rue's force boarded three train cars: one for his men, one for the horses and one for the artillery. Because Morgan had destroyed some of the tracks, Rue and his men had to transfer to a Baltimore & Ohio Railroad train that took them to Bellaire. From there, they took another train toward the Ohio River, leaving their artillery behind. At Steubenville, scouts reported that Morgan was headed to Salineville. Rue's force detrained and then rode for Wintersville.

Morgan saw Rue coming and tried to veer off, but Rue's men had fresher horses and, taking a shortcut, got in front of the Rebel force. Morgan then sent a representative who asked for Rue's surrender! (This was, according to one newspaper account, a joke.) Morgan claimed he'd already surrendered to a Captain Burdick, who'd promised to take him and his men to Cincinnati, where they'd be granted parole. Captain Burdick was a soldier in the Columbiana County militia. Rue had never heard of Burdick and told Morgan to fight or surrender. Morgan chose the latter.

Rue went to Morgan's camp to accept his surrender. As he headed there, he saw Morgan's men sleeping along the side of the road despite the heat. He noticed Morgan's stolen thoroughbred mare, which he reluctantly gave up. In his later recollection of the event, Rue wrote, "John Morgan was the

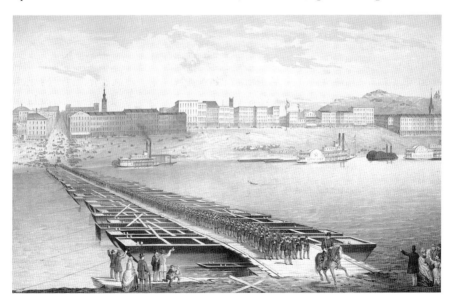

During the Civil War, Cincinnati was connected to Kentucky using pontoon bridges like this one sketched by A.E. Mathews, circa 1861–65. *Library of Congress.*

Morgan and his men were sent to the Ohio Penitentiary in Columbus (seen here circa 1900–6), from which they escaped by tunneling out. *Library of Congress.*

prince of horse thieves. He stole more horses than any other man who ever lived on earth."

Morgan's raid did accomplish its goal of diverting Union troops. Over 100,000 men were sent to apprehend him, allowing General Bragg to retreat and thus delay the fall of eastern Tennessee. Governor Tod calculated that it had cost the State of Ohio $212,381.97 to send its 587 militia companies after Morgan. Then there were the damages claimed by citizens. The Ohio legislature established a special commission to deal with these on March 30, 1864. Claims totaled $678,915.03. Of this, $493,372.76 was against Rebels, $172,319.67 against Union troops and $13,332.60 against Ohio's militias. Not a single claim against the Rebels was for gold or silver. Most of them were for stolen horses and saddles. Other claims included property damage and stolen food, liquor, tobacco and goods from stores.

Morgan and his officers were sent to the Ohio Penitentiary in Columbus. An escape plan was hatched. A tunnel was started in cell 19, the one occupied by Captain Thomas Hines. He and the others dug through the floor, placing a bed over the hole to keep it concealed. They used case-knives smuggled from the dining room and a stolen shovel to excavate. Not all of them could leave because their cells were too close to the watching eyes of guards. On November 27, 1863, Morgan, Hines, Ralph Sheldon, Samuel Taylor, Jacob Bennett, L.D. Hockersmith and Augustus Magee crawled through their tunnel and made their way to Confederate territory.

In July 1864, Morgan led an unsuccessful raid into Kentucky. He headed into eastern Tennessee in September of that same year. Union troops cornered him at Greeneville, Tennessee, on the fourteenth of that month. While trying to escape capture via a garden, he was shot in the back and killed by a private who'd previously served in the Confederate army.

CHAPTER 8

DANIEL M. BROWN'S CALIFORNIA GOLD

In 1850, Daniel M. Brown went to California, where he sold at a discount between $80,000 and $100,000 in counterfeit bills in exchange for gold dust, coins and nuggets. He took a ship to New York City and from there headed to his Ohio home in Summit County, where he died of an unspecified disease. On his heels were detectives who exhumed his body to make sure he was really dead. Only $20,000 was found. Brown was buried on his family farm.

Born in 1820, he was the son of the legendary counterfeiter James "Jim" Brown and raised in Cuyahoga Valley near the village of Boston. Many counterfeiters lived here because its caves, ravines and other natural hiding places made it the perfect place to keep out of sight from authorities. Counterfeiters were initially attracted to the location because the Ohio and Erie Canal ran through it, an artificial waterway that stretched 308 miles from Cleveland to Portsmouth. It connected the Great Lakes to the Ohio River, and on it counterfeit money could easily travel to New Orleans.

Dan Brown had his first known brush with the law in February 1838. He and a man named Rathburn were arrested for counterfeiting $20,000. They were caught on horseback in Medina County, and the officers who arrested them foolishly allowed their suspects to rub down their horses at a hotel stable before being searched, which is why nothing incriminating was found on their persons. Counterfeit money was buried in the straw in a horse stall. The suspects were locked in Elyria's jail, where Brown demonstrated his uncanny ability to escape imprisonment. He sawed through the irons confining him. A grand jury indicted Rathburn but not Brown.

Brown spent the next few years working along the Maumee River and in southeast Michigan. In 1842, counterfeit coins so good they were hard to detect started turning up in in Michigan's Oakland County, in which part of Detroit stood. This caught the attention of U.S. district attorney George C. Bates. Born in Canandaigua, New York, he studied in the law office of John C. Spencer. One of Bates's fellow students was Stephen A. Douglas, the man whose debates with upstart politician Abraham Lincoln made the latter famous throughout the country. Bates moved to Detroit in 1833 and was admitted to the bar the next year. He practiced law until being appointed district attorney by President William Henry Harrison, an office Bates held from 1841 to 1845.

Before setting off to investigate the source of the coins, Bates was alerted that a cask being shipped from Detroit to Cleveland had shifted dramatically when moved. It was put onto a ship bound for Cleveland and taken down the Ohio and Erie Canal to Portsmouth, where it would be delivered to a man named Daniel West. Bates had the cask opened. Within was a screw press used to mint coins plus all the paraphernalia needed for counterfeiting them. Bates ordered the cask repacked and a U.S. deputy marshal to keep an eye on it, but he lost track of it in Cleveland during the ship's unloading.

U.S. deputy marshal Thomas McKinstry had also heard of a coin minting machine on its way to Cleveland. He went to Brown's father, Jim, and asked him for the location. Jim said he'd only tell what McKinstry wanted to know if he helped Dan with his legal trouble in Detroit. McKinstry declined to make this deal.

In late September, a man named Cook arrived in Cleveland from Buffalo, New York. Bound for Pittsburgh, Pennsylvania, he was a bit short on money. He met Daniel West on board the canalboat *Hibernia*. West offered to advance him twenty-five dollars if he repaid him thirty dollars and took his trunk to Portsmouth. The boat's captain, R.D. Baxter, served as a witness to this transaction. On September 24, 1845, he turned the trunk over to West's care. West was an alias used by Daniel Brown.

Bates decided to investigate the source of the counterfeit coins in the rural part of Oakland County. To further the deception, he brought with him his wife and the son of U.S. marshal Joshua Howard from Detroit. Taking up the guise of a hunter, he found $40,000 or $50,000 in bad coins. Most were passed by farmers who'd been told by Brown and his accomplices that since the coins were nearly identical to real ones, it wasn't a crime to use them. Nine farmers were arrested and taken to Detroit, where a grand jury indicted them. All were tried and convicted. According to an account written

COINING PRESS.

Coining press, 1861. *Library of Congress.*

by Samuel A. Lane, who served for a time as the Summit County sheriff, two died in prison "of grief." A couple years later, several were pardoned by the president at the suggestion of the district attorney. The same grand jury that dealt with the farmers also indicted Brown for his scheme. He escaped with about $40,000, with $15,000 to $20,000 of it being good money.

Bates traced Brown to a hotel in St. Louis, Missouri, via a letter intercepted at the Detroit Post Office. He and a U.S. deputy marshal traveled to St. Louis and with a local detective went to the hotel in question. While signing the register, they noticed Dan West had checked in. The two asked if West was in at the moment. The clerk said he'd go find out. He departed via the kitchen and then took a steamboat down the Mississippi River headed for Little Rock, Arkansas. This clerk was Brown, who'd taken the place of the real clerk after he stepped out.

Bates returned to private practice in 1846. It was then that Brown's sister, a noted beauty and an excellent mimic, offered Bates her gold watch and $800 in gold as a retainer to defend her brother at his upcoming trial. To gain sympathy, she pointed out that the Brown family had some problems. Brown's wife, whom he married in 1845, suffered from poor health, and his father was in prison. Bates refused to take the retainer unless he met Brown in person, who was at the time hiding somewhere in Ohio. Bates told her that if he thought there was enough evidence for him to defend Brown, he'd take the retainer. If a jury found Brown not guilty, he'd earn another $1,000.

Lane wrote that Bates met Brown near Maumee in "a dismantled old brick stage house, about six miles out, on the Perrysburg pike, the house being kept by a repulsive old woman." Brown offered Bates punch poured into a silver goblet from a silver pitcher. Bates refused to drink until Brown did first. Brown said as a rule he didn't drink alcohol because it had ruined his father, which was why he now sat in a prison cell. Bates drank the punch.

Jim Brown had been convicted by the U.S. government for making thirty counterfeit U.S. mint half-dollar gold coins. A search of his house had unearthed the materials and tools used to make them. There was also paper for printing bank notes. At age sixty-six, Jim was sentenced to ten years' hard labor. Despite having been a counterfeiter for almost forty years, this was the only time he'd ever been convicted of a crime. He'd made a fortune counterfeiting, and at one point in his life, he'd amassed about $1 million. With this, he bought a three-hundred-acre farm and on that built a mansion. Like his son, Jim was over six feet tall. He had a head

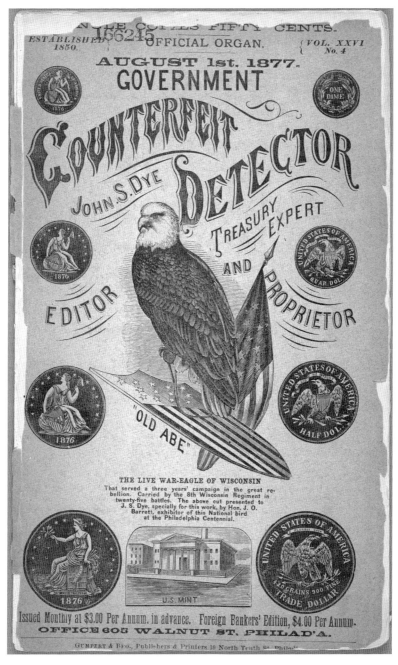

In nineteenth-century America, counterfeiting was such a large problem that periodicals like the *Government Counterfeit Detector* were produced to help people identify phony money. *New York Public Library Digital Collections.*

of white hair in his later years. Many fondly called him "Old Jim" and, less flattering, "Sly Jim." Neither he nor his son ever passed the money they made personally. Dan told Bates: "We are wholesale counterfeit coiners and only sell to retail dealers, who buy from us well-knowing that the coin is spurious." American counterfeiters rarely passed what they produced, a point to remember later.

The key witness against Dan Brown was his ex-lover living in Detroit. If she didn't testify against him, Bates promised an acquittal. But if the current U.S. district attorney for Michigan, John Norvell, found her, Brown was done for. Brown decided to stay on the run rather than face trial. He offered Bates a considerable amount of money as a retainer. Bates declined, pointing out he might one day be reappointed as U.S. district attorney. He took payment only for the meeting.

President Zachary Taylor made Bates an assistant U.S. district attorney in 1849. Bates decided to pursue Brown, but he never had the chance. Brown headed to Missouri, where he went by the alias Timothy Lacey. Indicted for counterfeiting, he made his way to California and its gold fields. It was the first year of the California Gold Rush.

Brown wasn't the only person from Summit County to seek his fortune here. Lane, in his history of the county, wrote that he and "two or three hundred" of its citizens headed to California. Among them was Dan's uncle

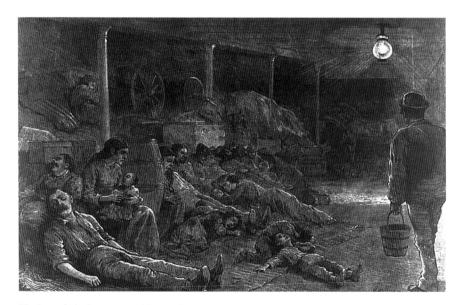

Victims of cholera, 1875. *Library of Congress.*

William T. Mather, a businessman from Akron who became seriously ill while in Sacramento. He'd likely contracted cholera.

Cholera originated in India. It is an intestinal disease that causes violent vomiting and diarrhea, which results in severe dehydration, killing about half of those who catch it. It first appeared in the United States in 1832 and was probably brought here from Europe by the British, who had gotten it from India. It disappeared from the United States until 1848, when cases erupted in New York City and New Orleans. It reached Sacramento in October 1850, and thousands fled the settlement in November. Cholera is transmitted in conditions where poor sanitation exists, something Sacramento had in abundance. Its population of ten thousand or so lived primarily in shacks and tents. There were about one hundred hotels and houses and a few crude hospitals.

After recovering, Mather made his way to San Francisco, where he met Lane. He told Lane that his nephew planned to take home between $75,000 and $80,000 in gold and silver coins and gold dust—at least if he lived long enough. Lane reported that Brown had tuberculosis and was doing poorly. Mather claimed that Brown had acquired his gold by personally passing crisp $50 and $100 bills from the Missouri State Bank, called "Pukes" by native Missourians.

There are problems with this accusation. Throughout his career, Brown specialized in coins, not paper money. That he passed the bills himself is exceeding unlikely. He told Bates he always sold to wholesalers, and they passed it. Most importantly, the real counterfeiters and the man who passed the bills in California were all caught, and there is nothing that indicates Brown had any association with this group.

The bank notes were engraved by Henry Lovejoy in St. Louis. According to the Washington, D.C. newspaper *National Intelligencer*, "A press, a copper plate for $10 notes of the Bank of Missouri, about $8,000 in unsigned notes, and a quantity of paper prepared for working were seized. Two persons were at work on the press when the arrest was made." They were Alvin Brown and a Mr. McAfee. The man who passed them to miners in California was George S. Moore.

Brown sailed from Sacramento to New York City. During the journey, his health deteriorated even more. Friends summoned by telegraph helped get him home. Knowing his time was short, he deeded the farm to his brother James Jr. on December 27, 1850. He arranged for his fortune to pass to others. He died on January 31, 1851, at age thirty-one. Some sources say he contracted scurvy, which is something many of those involved with

GOLD IN CALIFORNIA.—"EL DORADO," IN SACRAMENTO.—(SEE NEXT PAGE.)

"Gold in California—'El Dorado' in Sacramento," 1852. *Library of Congress.*

the California Gold Rush suffered from. Still, once back home, a diet of vitamin C would have reversed its effects, so it's more likely that tuberculosis killed him.

Just because Brown had nothing to do with the Missouri counterfeiting scheme doesn't mean he'd gone to California to make an honest living. While there, he'd swindled a number of people, prompting a committee to form and pursue him. Arriving in New York City, it traveled to Cleveland, where it learned that Brown was dead. The committee members traveled to Akron, where they met the physician who'd attended Brown's death, Alpheus Kilbourn, and the attorney, Rufus P. Spalding, who'd helped to settle Brown's affairs. A detective was among the committee members, and still unconvinced, he went to Brown's family and convinced them to exhume his quarry. This ended the pursuit for good.

It's always possible that Brown buried some of his ill-gotten gold somewhere on his farm or elsewhere in the Cuyahoga Valley, though it seems more likely he willed it to others. In any case, if anyone today digs up gold or money (real or fake), there's no guarantee it belonged to Brown. His family's farm was near Boston and the Yellow Creek, an area Ravenna's newspaper *Ohio Star* accused of being "infested with counterfeiters" such as Rinaldo D. Baxter.

In 1853, authorities visited this man's house and there met his wife. They told her they were on the run for passing some of Baxter's bills and hoped she'd hide them from the officers. She invited them in, fed them and let them stay the night. In the morning, they told his wife who they were. She broke down in tears. They searched her house but found nothing but a couple of counterfeit dimes. Searching the barn, which they practically tore apart, they found, according to the *Ohio Star*, "under the feed trough, nicely stowed away $13,433 of counterfeit money, mostly on the Ohio State Bank." The officers stayed at the house to await Baxter's return.

Another group of officers found Baxter in the nearby village of Boston the next morning. Not revealing their true purpose, they told him he was accused of being party to the beating of a canal man in Ravenna the night before. Baxter, knowing himself innocent, agreed to go with them to clear the matter up. They stopped at his house and there revealed their true purpose: he was under arrest for counterfeiting. Furious, he threatened to kill them all but in the end parted from his wife and four children without a fight.

CHAPTER 9

THE VAULT OF GEORGE REMUS

The Eighteenth Amendment prohibited the "manufacture, sale, or transportation of intoxicating liquors" in the United States. On January 17, 1920, Congress passed the Volstead Act to give it teeth. President Woodrow Wilson vetoed this law, but Congress overrode it. The law had loopholes that George Remus, a lawyer from Chicago, Illinois, decided to exploit to his own advantage. He set up shop in the Cincinnati area and stashed much of his illegal alcohol at a farm called Death Valley. It was here, or possibly in Tug Fork, Kentucky, where he had a secret vault constructed in which he stored millions of dollars. He never revealed its location.

Remus biographer William A. Cook wrote that Remus was born on November 14, 1874, and that his family came to America in 1879, but Remus once stated during a congressional hearing that he was born in Germany on November 13, 1876, and moved to the United States at the age of four. His family settled in Baltimore, Maryland, in 1880; briefly moved to Milwaukee, Wisconsin; and then settled in Chicago. Remus quit school in 1890 and went to work at his uncle's pharmacy to help support the family after his father, Frank, stopped working because of rheumatism. George attended the Chicago College of Pharmacy to learn this profession. Lying about his age—he was just nineteen—he passed the state examination for a pharmacist's license. At twenty-one, he bought his uncle's pharmacy, and within five years, he had purchased a second one.

He married Lillian Klauff on July 10, 1899, with whom he had a daughter, Romola. A short, pudgy man known for his temper and use of fists, he sometimes referred to himself in the third person. Having gone into the pharmacy business out of necessity and not preference, he decided he'd like to become a lawyer and to that end started attending night school. Admitted to the bar in 1900, he opened his own law practice.

In 1916, he met Augusta Imogene Holmes (who went by her middle name), a worker at a delicatessen in the process of getting a divorce. The two engaged in an affair. Remus's wife filed for divorce on March 7, 1919. Her divorce complaint said that her husband had provided a home for his mistress for the past three years, and he'd allegedly beat her with his fists. In the divorce settlement, she received a lump sum of $50,000 plus lifelong alimony. Romola received $30,000. Remus married Imogene on June 25, 1920, and adopted her thirteen-year-old daughter, Ruth.

Remus never drank or smoked, but he had no issue with people who did. After Prohibition took effect, he began representing clients who'd violated the Volstead Act. Those who lost often received fines as high as $10,000, but rather than complain, many paid up on the spot either with war bonds or wads of cash that included thousand-dollar bills. Remus made $50,000 a year, a good living, but he realized he'd make a whole lot more if he went into the bootlegging business. He decided to exploit a legal loophole to do it.

Under the Volstead Act, any alcoholic beverages a person possessed before Prohibition went into effect could be kept save in states that passed laws making its possession illegal. Likewise, while the unsold liquor produced by distilleries couldn't be sold on the open market, it still belonged to the companies that produced it. It was stored in bonded government warehouses, a practice that traces its roots to the Civil War. To help pay for that conflict, the federal government imposed a tax on every gallon of liquor sold. At first, distilled spirits that had to be aged like brandy, whiskey and rum were taxed on what was produced, but distillers complained that during the aging process, barrels lost between two and three gallons. The government rectified this by storing the barrels in a bonded warehouse and only taxing the amount sold.

Under the Volstead Act, spirits in bonded warehouses could be sold legally for medicinal purposes so long as doctors filled out special government-issued prescriptions. In the first six months of 1920, 150,000 physicians applied for these, which were quickly counterfeited and forged. The government continuously updated them to prevent this, but it was an effort in futility.

Those who sold the liquor to the pharmacies filling these prescriptions needed to obtain wholesale withdraw permits. Remus's plan was to obtain permits, buy the liquor in bonded warehouses and then sell it to drugstores as medicinal alcohol. It sounded legal, and had he strictly adhered to the

Photos like this showing agents of New York deputy commissioner John A. Leach (*right*) overseeing liquor being poured into a sewer, circa 1921, were good for publicity, but the reality was that much of the nation's liquor was in private hands and not subject to this kind of treatment. *Library of Congress.*

model, he might have gotten away with it. At a congressional hearing, Senator Burton K. Wheeler of Montana asked Remus what he thought of prescriptions for medicinal alcohol. Remus answered, "It is the greatest comedy, the greatest perversion of justice, that I have ever known of in any civilized country in the world." To this, Wheeler agreed.

Remus began his enterprise by purchasing small amounts of whiskey, but this brought the unwanted attention of Chicago's criminal underworld. Suddenly, federal agents raided the building in which he had his law office, claiming to have found fifteen barrels of whiskey that had been withdrawn using false permits from the Sibley Warehouse and Storehouse Company. Remus was charged for this alleged crime and released on a $10,000 bond. After he failed to show up at court, an arrest warrant was issued, but the case was ultimately dropped.

This government-bonded warehouse was on the property of the Maker's Mark Distillery near Loretto, Kentucky. *Library of Congress.*

Because most distilled liquor in the United States was stored within a three-hundred-mile radius of Cincinnati, Remus decided to relocate there. Before finding a permanent residence, he stayed at the Sinton Hotel. He built a relationship with local banker Oscar Fender of the Lincoln National Bank and then deposited $100,000 into it. The first distillery he purchased was the Edgewood in Cincinnati. As his operations expanded, he purchased more distilleries in Ohio, Kentucky and Indiana. To acquire the needed withdrawal permits, he bought the Kentucky Drug Company, to which not a drop of liquor ever went. He founded a transportation company and stored all his booze in Death Valley.

This consisted of fifty acres of land bought from George Dater located ten miles from Cincinnati. In the February 1929 issue of *True Detective Magazine*, writer Mary Chenoweth described it as "a concentration camp," a type of prison invented by the Spanish to house Cuban dissidents without trial that in 1929 hadn't yet become associated with the Nazis. From the road, hundreds of pear trees hid the main house and outbuildings. To get to them, vehicles descended a steep grade. Death Valley had roaming guards armed with repeating rifles. Their aim wasn't to stop government agents from raiding the place but rather to protect it against whiskey pirates.

Behind the two-story house was a "deep hollow concealed by trees" where between five thousand and twenty thousand cases of whiskey were stored. More was put in the outbuildings and a barn. When space ran out, Remus and one of his lieutenants, George Connors, secretly excavated a cellar only accessible through a trapdoor that was hidden by hay. Possibly this is the "hidden vault" that treasure hunters have heard about. On one day alone, sales from Death Valley amounted to $79,000. During the nineteen months of his bootlegging career, Remus made an estimated $6.7 million.

His operation was known as The Circle. And despite its sheen of legality, it was as crooked as any other bootlegging enterprise. Remus employed "confidence men" to trick law enforcement agents to accept bribes. His "traffic man" helped to organize transportation. Others forged documents for his operation. He employed George Connors as chauffeur and personal cook, but this man was really a loyal top lieutenant who did anything that Remus needed. Connors was by profession a real estate agent who met Remus during that latter's buying spree of distilleries. Imogene and her brother, George Brown, also had important roles in the organization.

Sometimes Remus bought the stock from distilleries and not the whole business. One example of this was the Jack Daniel's warehouse in St. Louis, Missouri. Jack Daniel's Distillery was founded shortly after the Civil War by Jasper "Jack" Newton Daniel in Lynchburg, Tennessee. Dying in 1911, he left the company to his nephew Lemuel Motlow. Realizing the temperance movement was gaining popularity in rural Tennessee where Lynchburg was located, Motlow decided to move operations to St. Louis.

When Prohibition took effect, 893 barrels of the company's top-quality whiskey were stored in its St. Louis warehouse. In the spring of 1923, St. Louis broker R.A. Organ, who represented Don H. Robinson and his partners, offered to buy all the barrels in the city plus stock the company had stored in its Cincinnati and Birmingham, Alabama, warehouses. Motlow and his partners, Harry L. Dahlman and Thomas A. Hefferman, had a counterproposal: they'd sell their whiskey, warehouses and the distillery for $400,000. Robinson and his partners only wanted the whiskey, so further negotiations facilitated by their attorney, Remus, took place.

In the deal, finalized on June 26, 1923, Remus and other investors paid $125,000 for the stock in the St. Louis warehouse plus that in Cincinnati and Birmingham—exactly what they wanted in the first place. Remus, who contributed $50,000, helped bribe the right people. St. Louis politician Jack Kratz made sure the Internal Revenue Service didn't interfere in exchange for receiving $12 for every case sold. Deputy gauger William J. Kinney received $3 a case. The local police were paid to look the other way.

Motlow and his partners thought they were dealing with legitimate businessmen, not bootleggers. Robinson leased the St. Louis warehouse for $500 a month. Remus arranged for the liquor to be secretly transported to Cincinnati. On August 23, 1923, thirty thousand gallons were siphoned off, put into barrels and placed onto waiting trucks. The original plan was to replace it with cheaper whiskey, but none was to be had, so water was used. On the evening of September 9, 1923, Charles Barlow and night watchman Henry Fink decided to sample the wares. To their surprise, they found it was just "sour water."

The Jack Daniel's operation would cause Remus headaches later, but not as much as his purchase of the Squibb Distillery in Lawrenceburg, Indiana. It resided in territory policed under the command of the incorruptible Bert C. Morgan, who was known as the "Bloodhound of the Prohibition Force." When Squibb's liquor started showing up on the bootleg market, he ordered his men to watch the distillery. He knew the Cincinnati Ring was involved because many times seized whiskey bottles were wrapped in Cincinnati newspapers, but he had no idea who ran the organization. The arrest of a bootlegger in Hammond, Indiana, changed all that. This fellow revealed where the liquor was coming from: Death Valley near Cheviot, Ohio.

Morgan forwarded this intelligence to the Prohibition chief in charge of that region, Gus Simmons, and he ordered the raid on Death Valley Farm on October 22, 1921. According to a newspaper account that appeared in the Hammond newspaper *Lake County Times*, the raid seized "600 gallons of whiskey, 46 packages of assorted liquors, 800 gallons of port and white wine, 23 quarts of old Dearborn whiskey, 11 quarts of Vermouth, [and] 36 quarts of gin." Most of it was stored in barrels fresh from distilleries. Also on the premises was a bottling plant.

Multiple agents began investigating Remus for different crimes. He and thirteen others were indicted by a federal grand jury in Indiana on April 22, 1922, for violating various Prohibition laws. Former Prohibition agent R.E. Flora was charged with the disappearance of permits from a safe in a federal building that had been used to withdraw liquor from the Squibb Distillery's warehouse in Lawrenceburg. Remus was also charged with attempting to bribe Prohibition agents, one of whom was Morgan. Remus had offered him half a million dollars to look the other way.

Held in May, the trial was in Cincinnati. The jury found Remus guilty of conspiracy to violate national Prohibition laws and attempting to bribe

Bottling plant at Maker's Mark Distillery. *Library of Congress.*

Morgan. He was fined $10,000 and sentenced to two years in federal prison. Sent to the United States Penitentiary in Atlanta, Georgia, he gave the power of attorney to Imogene to administer his fortune.

He didn't do well in prison. By the seventh month, he decided to give up others in order to get out. Told that Bureau of Investigation agent Franklin L. Dodge would be willing to listen to what he had to reveal, Remus asked Imogene to contact him. Dodge, who came from Lansing, Michigan, contacted her first. He was investigating the robbery of the Jack Daniel's warehouse. A tall, good-looking man, he and Imogene quickly fell in love. Dodge convinced Imogene it was in her best interest that her husband stay in prison for his full sentence, which he did.

Released on August 25, 1925, Remus saw no sign of Imogene. Instead, he was greeted by a U.S. marshal carrying an arrest warrant. He took Remus to a St. Louis jail, where he'd await trial for the robbery of the Jack Daniel's warehouse. He was given a bond of $50,000, and not a soul came to bail him out despite his claim that local politicians owed him over $400,000. He made bail by putting up an office building he owned in Cincinnati as collateral.

Entrance to the federal penitentiary in Atlanta, 1910. *Library of Congress.*

None of his local business associates involved in the Jack Daniel's theft wanted anything to do with him, so he traveled to Washington, D.C., to visit the woman who'd put him in prison in the first place: Assistant District Attorney Mabel Walker Willebrandt. He offered to tell her everything about the robbery of the Jack Daniel's warehouse in exchange for immunity. To this, Willebrandt agreed.

The trial was held in Indianapolis, Indiana. Remus feared for his life and demanded police protection, which he received. This wasn't paranoia. Some dangerous people were involved. He stayed at the Claypool Hotel in a room next to the one occupied by Special District Attorney John R. Marshall. Also staying in the hotel were Imogene and Dodge. While on his way to dinner, Remus saw Dodge and tried to attack him.

Someone did try to have Remus killed, but it wasn't one of his former business associates; it was Imogene and Dodge. They hired Harry Truesdale, a native of Hamilton, Ohio, to do the deed, a task for which he was ill suited. He later testified that they paid him $10,000 to kill Imogene's estranged husband. A petty thief rather than a hardened criminal, Truesdale and Imogene went to the Grand Hotel to find her husband, but he wasn't there. Imogene was armed with a pistol and said she'd kill Remus herself given the chance. Truesdale decided that if Imogene and Dodge were willing to kill Remus, they'd probably betray him, so the next day, he told Remus about the whole scheme. Another source says a journalist told Remus about the plot.

Imogene was indicted in the Jack Daniel's case, but charges against her were dropped. Others weren't so lucky. Twenty defendants from St. Louis and three from Cincinnati were found guilty of conspiracy to violate federal Prohibition laws.

Remus had more legal troubles to deal with. Death Valley Farm was declared a nuisance, and he was charged as the one responsible for this. Found guilty, he spent another year in an Ohio jail. He also faced possible deportation. Imogene told immigration authorities that his father hadn't become a U.S. citizen, meaning that none of his children had, either. Remus defeated the deportation attempt.

Upon Remus's completion of his jail sentence on April 26, 1927, Connors picked him up and drove him to his Cincinnati house. Within, Remus found little save for some rubbish and a few items of no real value. Imogene had auctioned everything off for well under its real value. When writer Mary Chenoweth asked Remus about this incident, he wept. Imogene and Dodge liquidated and hid most of Remus's fortune, leaving him with nothing. Dodge sold all of Remus's liquor withdraw permits. In a deposition filed in

This is the largest illegal still captured by federal agents during Prohibition. *From left to right:* Lieutenant O.T. Davis, Sergeant J.D. McQuade, George Fowler of the IRS and H.G. Bauer, November 11, 1922. *Library of Congress.*

Cincinnati's Court of Domestic Relations, Remus claimed Imogene had $2 million of his money. He hired detectives to find her, but they had no luck.

Imogene returned to Cincinnati, where she filed for divorce. At eight o'clock in the morning of October 6, 1927, at the Alms Hotel, she and daughter Ruth got into a cab driven by Charles Stevens. Imogene told him to take her to the office of Edward T. Dixon, her divorce lawyer. A large touring car followed. Soon it forced the taxi off the road by the Eden Park greenhouse. The moment Stevens stopped, Remus jumped out of the touring car. Imogene told Stevens to get moving. The touring car pursued and stopped the taxi at the reservoir.

Ruth tried to get out, but her mother restrained her and then got out herself. Imogene tried to run, but Remus caught up with her, grabbing her by the right wrist. The two struggled. Remus put a pistol against her body, fired and then dropped her to the ground and fled. His car was driven by his chauffeur, George Klug. Imogene was taken to Bethesda Hospital, where she died at 10:45 a.m. Within half an hour of her death, Remus surrendered to police. One of the officers there, Lieutenant Kigan, told Remus his wife had died and asked what he thought about that. Remus answered, "She who dances down the primrose path must die on the primrose path. I'm happy. This is the first peace of mind I've had in two years."

Now Remus desperately needed money. Connors learned that there was a safety deposit box supposedly filled with some of his bonds, stocks and withdraw permits worth $1,800,000 in a Lansing bank. He'd learned that it had been twice visited by Dodge and a woman named A.H. Holmes, an alias being used by Imogene. Remus's lawyer, Charleston Elston, compelled the bank to open the box with a court order. Journalists and Michigan officials came to observe this, the latter hoping to take a percentage in taxes. All were disappointed. The box was empty.

Charged with murder, Remus pleaded temporary insanity. The jury of two women and ten men believed Remus killed his wife because of her affair with Dodge. It took just nineteen minutes for them to find Remus not guilty. Afterward, they congratulated him for getting off.

This didn't end the matter. The presiding judge, Chester R. Short, had told the jury this verdict wouldn't allow Remus to walk out of the courtroom a free man. A probate court presided over by Judge William H. Lueders still had to decide on the state of Remus's mental health. It declared him insane and sent him to the Lima State Mental Hospital for the Criminally Insane. An appeals court declared him sane and ordered his release. State attorneys immediately asked for and received a stay from the Ohio Supreme Court to keep him locked up. It declined Remus's request for bail. On a later date, the Supreme Court examined the Court of Appeals' decision and ruled in favor of Remus in a four-to-three decision. Released near the end of June 1928, he went home to Cincinnati.

While he didn't return to the bootlegging business, he did sue multiple associates in an effort to regain some of his lost fortune. This effort failed. If he ever had a fortune stashed in a hidden vault, it was long gone by this point. He married for a third time, this time to Blanche Watson, and the two had a quiet life. In his last years, he lived in a boardinghouse in Covington, Kentucky, under the care of a nurse. He died on January 20, 1952, and was buried in Falmouth, Kentucky.

CHAPTER 10

TREASURE IN
THE DEPTHS BELOW

Estimates of the number of sunken watercrafts in the shallow depths of Lake Erie range from 1,400 to 2,000. Some are said to have gone down carrying a considerable fortune in either cargo or, more tantalizing for treasure hunters, gold. In his 1976 book *A Guide to Treasure in Michigan and Ohio*, Michael Paul Henson wrote about several of these "treasure ships." One was the sidewheel steamer *Chesapeake*, which sank three to four miles north of Conneaut. She supposedly had on board $8,000 in gold specie. Another source, Thomas P. Terry's *Great Lakes Treasure Wreck Atlas*, listed the value at $16,000, though he'd probably adjusted for inflation.

Just after midnight on June 15, 1847, the schooner *John A. Porter* maneuvered to avoid colliding with one vessel only to ram the *Chesapeake* in her port bow. The *John A. Porter*'s pilot later said he mistook the *Chesapeake*'s lights for those from shore. During the collision, several of the *John A. Porter*'s crewmen jumped on board the *Chesapeake*. The *Chesapeake*'s commander, Captain N.H. Warner, put them in his vessel's boat with the intent of sending them back to the *John A. Porter*, but the latter unexpectedly sank before they reached her.

The *Chesapeake* wasn't in much better shape, taking on far more water than her pumps and bailing could handle. Captain Warner put on all steam and headed for land with the idea of beaching his vessel. About a mile to a mile and a half from Conneaut, incoming water put her boiler fires out, stopping her dead. She had between forty and fifty passengers, many of them women and children. Ten were put into a boat and sent to shore. Mrs. Daniel Folsom initially refused to be one of its passengers but changed her mind when her husband put their child on board. Mr. Folsom and a friend floated for a time on a plank. The two separated, and Folsom was never heard from again.

The *Chesapeake* sank within half an hour of the collision in forty feet of water, or at least part of her did. The upper deck separated from the hull, staying afloat until around three o'clock in the morning. Captain Warner advised passengers to stay put rather than risk going it alone using a door or plank as a floating device. Most listened, but at least nine didn't, and it's they who drowned. Other unregistered passengers might have also perished. The shrieks of those on board failed to attract the attention of the passing vessel *Harrison*, which continued onward and docked at Conneaut.

High winds and waves forced the *Chesapeake*'s boat off course, causing it to land two miles from Conneaut's pier. Mr. Shepherd, the *Chesapeake*'s clerk, ran up the beach and reached the pier just as the *Harrison* docked. He informed her commander, Captain Parker, of the *Chesapeake*'s plight, so Parker took the *Harrison* back out to rescue who he could. A small boat also went out. In addition to Folsom, those known to have drowned were George Van Doren, Mrs. Hock, E. Conn, S. York, First Engineer R. Sutherland, Second Porter G. Wait and a deckhand, R. McMann.

Their baggage wasn't as lucky. Not a single trunk was saved. None of the *Chesapeake*'s cargo was recovered, including about thirty tons of freight that consisted mainly of dry goods and groceries bound for Sandusky, as well as $8,000 in money. The idea that the money was gold specie probably came from the 1856 book *Lloyd's Steamboat Directory, and Disasters on the Western Waters*. Other than that, there's no evidence to suggest it was gold, and in the year of the *Chesapeake*'s loss, large amounts of this precious metal were rare in the United States. Probably the $8,000 was in paper money. The *Chesapeake*'s logs and accounting books would resolve this question, but they went down with her. The ship's cargo has never been found.

This isn't the only sunken Lake Erie vessel associated with Conneaut. The *Marquette & Bessemer No. 2*, which made the city its home port, is said to have been carrying gold when she went down on December 7, 1909. A ferry, she regularly sailed between Conneaut and Ontario's Port Stanley carrying the coal-filled rail cars of the Bessemer and Lake Erie Railroad. After unloading, they were connected to the Pere Marquette Railroad and taken to their final destination.

In the early 1800s, the only vessels in Conneaut's harbor were fishing boats docked at a small wooden pier or tied to pilings jutting out of the water. On shore stood just a few buildings. As late as 1871, the maximum draft of vessels entering the harbor without striking bottom was eleven feet.

Marquette & Bessemer No. 2. Wikimedia Commons.

Pere Marquette station in Charlevoix, Michigan. Detroit Publishing Co., circa 1900–6. *Library of Congress.*

Unloading ore at Conneaut Harbor. Detroit Publishing Co., circa 1900–6. *Library of Congress.*

Iron ore changed all that. By the 1870s, large quantities of it from Michigan was making its way south via Lake Erie. Once it was unloaded at a port, railroads took it to mills hungry for it.

In 1892, a railroad connection to Conneaut prompted Congress to authorize the work needed to deepen Conneaut's harbor so it could accommodate large ore ships. Not willing to wait for the funding, the Pittsburgh, Shenango and Lake Erie Railroad received permission to fix the piers and dredge the harbor to a depth of sixteen feet. The first ore ship to dock, *Charles J. Kershaw,* arrived on November 9, 1892. The Pittsburgh and Conneaut Dock Company incorporated in West Virginia on February 4, 1893, with the purpose of maintaining and controlling all aspects of the docks, harbor facilities and ships, plus the loading and unloading of ore and coal.

One of the vessels the company tended to, the *Marquette & Bessemer No. 2,* was owned and operated by the Marquette and Bessemer Dock and Navigation Company. Laid down in 1905 by the American Shipbuilding

"The Coming Storm, Lake Erie," 1926. *Library of Congress.*

Company in Cleveland and made of steel, the ship was 350 feet long with a 54-foot beam built for around $350,000. For reasons unknown, American Shipbuilding declined to give it a stern door to keep water out. Two weeks before the ship's disappearance, she almost went down for this reason. Her captain, Robert Rowan McLeod, nearly pushed several railcars overboard to lighten the load and then decided not to when the pumps got ahead of the incoming water.

McLeod, a native of Kincardine, Ontario, was born on October 3, 1862. His parents both emigrated from Scotland, meeting and marrying in Woodstock, Canada. Robert started his freshwater sailing career as an assistant cook on board the schooner *Maple Leaf* in 1874. Over the years, he worked his way up the ranks on a wide variety of vessels, as did his four brothers. Volume 2 of the 1899 book *History of the Great Lakes* noted that McLeod was "one of the few lake masters who have made a success of winter navigation, in which he has been engaged in the interests of railroad companies for the last ten years."

At 10:25 a.m. on December 7, 1909, the *Marquette* began her departure from Conneaut for her regular five- to six-hour run to Port Stanley. She had on board thirty railcars filled mainly with coal. Just as the ship pulled away from the pier, a man came running after and hailing her. This was Albert J. Weiss, the treasurer of the Keystone Fish Company of Erie, Pennsylvania. In a briefcase, he carried $50,000 to buy a shipment of fish

Conneaut Harbor. Detroit Publishing Co., circa 1900. *Library of Congress.*

from a Canadian company. The *Marquette* reversed her engines, and he boarded as her sole passenger.

Thirty-one crewmen were on board that day, including Captain McLeod and his first mate and brother, John. A good number of the *Marquette*'s crew lived in Conneaut, many of them having been born there. Some newspapers reported the number on board that day as thirty-eight, but the ship's owners later corrected that number, saying that six crewmen listed on the December 1 payroll from which this number came weren't on board that day.

As the *Marquette* steamed toward Port Stanley, a storm blew in. The temperature at Conneaut dropped from forty degrees Fahrenheit in the morning to zero at five o'clock in the afternoon. Winds blew as high as seventy miles per hour, whipping up massive waves. The addition of snow made it a blizzard. A tugboat saw the *Marquette* in the afternoon, and a Canadian customs office sighted her at Port Stanley's harbor entrance, into which she was unable to go because of the high waves. The *Marquette* headed toward Rondeau, Ontario. Some thought she was sheltering at Ontario's Long Point.

When she failed to show up the next day, tugs were sent out to search for her despite the fact that the weather hadn't improved. Among those that went was the *Commodore Perry* under the command of Captain Jeremy Driscoll. The

Commodore Perry came across flotsam from the *Marquette* that included tables, hatches and chairs. At about eleven o'clock in the morning on December 12, something in the distance caught Driscoll's eye. It turned out to be a green yawl from the missing ferry. Nine of the *Marquette*'s crewmen were found aboard, all frozen. This was Lifeboat 4, which could accommodate up to ten passengers and would have been the last one to be launched.

The smallest man on board, Manuel Souars, had no lifebelt on and lay beneath a seat with four men on top of his legs and lower body, presumably to keep him warm. All wore nothing but their work clothes save for the second cook, Harry Thomas, who had on an overcoat. This suggested that *Marquette* went under so fast they didn't have time to grab their weather gear. The heads of Thomas and O'Hagan, who sat upright, were covered with bruises and blood. Doubtless they'd been repeatedly slammed against the boat's side before perishing. The steward, George R. Smith, had grabbed his valuable galley knives and a meat cleaver. The others on board were Charles Allen Alsace, John "Paddy" Hart, Tom Steel and Joe Shenk (or possibly Shank).

The clothes of a tenth man were found in the lifeboat's bow. The newspaper article from which this information comes speculated that he went mad and jumped overboard. This is quite possible. Symptoms of severe hypothermia include sweating, feeling exceedingly warm and something known as "paradoxical undressing," which is exactly what it sounds like. Severe disorientation is another symptom. Because of the weather and rough seas, the crew of the *Commodore Perry* was unable to board the lifeboat, so it was towed in with a deckhand using a pike pole to keep it upright.

On the same day as this gruesome discovery, it was reported that part of the *Marquette* and several of her railcars were found under the ice at Port Bruce, Ontario, which is about fourteen miles from Port Stanley. The tug *Reed* reported seeing the wreck about twelve miles north of the Waldameer Resort in Erie, but this was dismissed as unlikely by the *Marquette*'s owners. The tug *Winner* reported the discovery of another lifeboat with bodies in it east of Port Burwell, Ontario. A lifeboat was later found in that vicinity, but no one was on board. In the spring, a third lifeboat was found smashed in two along a breakwater's rocks in the harbor at Buffalo, New York. The bodies of Chief Engineer Eugene Wood and oiler Patrick Keith were discovered a few months later.

Workers at the Niagara Power Company at Long Point came across John McLeod's body on April 6, 1910. He wore a *Marquette* lifebelt and had on his person $122, some documents and a card ID. The body of wheelsman

William Wilson also washed up here. Captain Robert McLeod's badly decomposed body was found on October 2 of that same year. Only his head and upper body remained. He was identified by the word "McLeod" tattooed on one of his arms.

What makes the *Marquette*'s sinking so remarkable isn't why she foundered— she probably sank after being swamped by water coming over her stern or was rolled over by a big wave—but rather why no one has ever found the ship. She was a large vessel, and Lake Erie is relatively shallow. Possibly she broke up and is scattered over a long portion of the lakebed, making her harder to find and easier for sand and silt to cover her remains.

The story of Albert J. Weiss carrying $50,000 to buy a fishing company is based on some truth. He did go to Canada to buy a shipment of fish, not an entire company. Weiss was the treasurer of his company, and he did seem rather keen to get to his destination that day, so it wouldn't be beyond reason that he did have a large amount of money with him for some kind of business transaction. If someone does find the wreck, it's unlikely any of the money he carried would be usable.

BIBLIOGRAPHY

Databases

California Digital Newspaper Collection
Chronicling America
Digital Michigan Libraries
EBSCO: Academic Search Premier
Elgin County Archives: Heritage Collections Elgin-St. Thomas
GALE: Nineteenth-Century U.S. Newspapers
JSTOR
Newsbank: America's News
Ohio Memory
ProQuest Historical Newspapers: New York Times
Richland Library (Mansfield, OH): Community History Archive
Stark Library (Canton, OH) newspaper database

American National Biography (Electronic Version)

Adams, Michael C. "Burnside, Ambrose Everett."
Gale, Robert L. "Dillinger, John."
Rosenburg, R.B. "Morgan, John Hunt."

Dictionary of Canadian Biography (Electronic Version)

Bosher, J.F., and J.-C. Dubé. "Bigot, François."

C té, Pierre-L. "Duquesne (du Quesne, Duqaine, Duqu ne) De Menneville, Ange, Marquis Duquesne."

Eccles, W.J. "Marin de la Malgue (la Marque), Paul."

Grenier, Fernand. "Pécaudy de Contrecoeur, Claude-Pierre."

Hunter, William A. "Tanaghrisson."

Taillemite, Étienne. "Dumas, Jean-Daniel."

Books

Abbott, Karen. *The Ghosts of Eden Park: The Bootleg King, the Women Who Pursued Him, and the Murder That Shocked Jazz-Age America.* New York: Crown, 2019.

Alvord, Clarence Walworth, ed. *Collections of the Illinois State Historical Library.* Springfield, IL: Trustees of the Illinois State Historical Library, 1908.

Beaver, Roy C. *The Bessemer and Lake Erie Railroad: 1869–1969.* San Marino, CA: Golden West Books, 1969.

Boyer, Dwight. *Ghost Ships of the Great Lakes.* Cleveland, OH: Freshwater Press, 1968.

Chernow, Ron. *Washington: A Life.* New York: Penguin Books, 2010.

Cook, William A. *King of the Bootleggers: A Biography of George Remus.* Jefferson, NC: McFarland & Company, 2008.

Cordingly, David. *Under the Black Flag: The Romance and the Reality of Life Among the Pirates.* San Diego: Harcourt Brace & Company, 1995.

Cromie, Robert, and Joseph Pinkston. *Dillinger: A Short and Violent Life.* Evanston, IL: Chicago Historical Bookworks, 1990.

Davies, Owen. *Grimoires: A History of Magic Books.* New York: Oxford University Press, 2009.

Duke, Basil. *History of Morgan's Cavalry.* Cincinnati, OH: Miami Printing and Publishing Company, 1867.

Dye, John S. *The Government Blue-Book: A Complete History of the Lives of All the Great Counterfeiters, Criminal Engravers and Plate Printers.* Philadelphia: Dye's Government Counterfeit Detector, 1880.

Early History of Michigan with Biographies of State Officers, Members of Congress, Judges and Legislators. Lansing, MI: Thorp & Godfrey, 1888.

Ervin, Robert E. *The John Morgan Hunt Raid of 1863.* Jackson, OH: Robert Edgar Ervin with assistance from the Jackson County Historical Society, 2003.

Fairburn, William Armstrong. *Merchant Sail*. Vol. 2. Center Lovell: Fairburn Maine Educational Foundation, 1945–55.

Girardin, G. Russell, with William J. Helmer. *Dillinger: The Untold Story*. Bloomington: Indiana State University, 1994.

Gorn, Elliot J. *Dillinger's Wild Ride: The Year That Made America's Public Enemy Number One*. New York: Oxford University Press, 2009.

Hamilton, Charles, ed. *Braddock's Defeat: The Journal of Captain Robert Cholmley's Batman, the Journal of a British Officer, Halkett's Orderly Book*. Norman: University of Oklahoma Press, 1959.

Henson, Michael Paul. *A Guide to Treasure in Michigan and Ohio*. Conroe, TX: Carter/Latham Publishing Company, 1976.

History of Clinton County, Indiana, Together with Sketches of Its Cities, Villages and Towns, Educational, Religious, Civil, Military and Political History, Portraits of Prominent Persons, and Biographies of Representative Citizens. Chicago: Inter-State Publishing Co., 1886.

History of Van Wert and Mercer Counties, Ohio with Illustrations and Biographical Sketches of Some of Its Prominent Men and Pioneers. Wapakoneta, OH: R. Sutton & Co., 1882.

Lane, Samuel A. *Fifty Years and Over of Akron and Summit County*. Akron, OH: Beacon Job Department, 1862.

Lehman, John H. *A Standard History of Stark County, Ohio: An Authentic Narrative of the Past, with Particular Attentions to the Modern Era in the Commercial, Industrial, Civic and Social Development…* Vol. 1. Chicago: Lewis Publishing Company, 1916.

Lloyd, James T. *Lloyd's Steamboat Directory, and Disasters on the Western Waters…* Cincinnati, OH: James T. Lloyd & Co., 1856.

Mansfield, John Brandt. *History of the Great Lakes*. Vols. 1 & 2. Chicago: J.H. Beers & Co., 1899.

Manuscript Records of the French and Indian War in the Library of the Society. Worcester, MA: American Antiquarian Society, 1909.

Marvel, William. *Burnside*. Chapel Hill: University of North Carolina Press, 1991.

McCardell, Lee. *Ill-Starred General: Braddock of the Coldstream Guards*. Pittsburgh, PA: University of Pittsburgh Press, 1958.

McLean, John. *Reports of Cases Argued and Decided in the Circuit Court of the United States, for the Seventh Circuit*. Vol. 4. Cincinnati, OH: H.W. Derby & Co., 1851.

Mihm, Stephen. *A Nation of Counterfeiters: Capitalists, Con Men, and the Making of the United States*. Cambridge, MA: Harvard University Press, 2007.

Morgan, Dan J. *Historical Lights and Shadows of the Ohio Penitentiary and the Horrors of the Death Trap: Heart-Rending Scenes and Sad Wailings, as Wife Parts with Husband, and Weeping Children Kiss a Doomed Father for the Last Time.* Columbus, OH: Hann & Adair, 1899.

Peet, Stephen D. *The Ashtabula Disaster.* Chicago: J.S. Goodman, 1877.

Pinkerton, Allan. *Thirty Years a Detective: Through a Comprehensive Exposé of Criminal Practices of All Grades and Classes Containing Numerous Episodes of Personal Experience in the Detection of Criminals, and Covering a Period of Thirty Years' Active Detective Life.* New York: G.W. Dillingham Co., 1884.

Portrait and Biographical Record of Stark County, Ohio, Containing Biographical Sketches of Prominent Representative Citizens, Together with Biographies of All the Presidents of the United States. Chicago: Chapman Bros., 1892.

Roose, William. *Indiana's Birthplace: A History of Harrison County[,] Indiana.* New Albany, IN: Tribune Company, 1911.

Sanderson, Thomas W., ed. *20th Century History of Youngstown and Mahoning County, Ohio, and Representative Citizens.* Chicago: Biographical Publishing Company, 1907.

Siedel, Frank. *Out of the Midwest: More Chapters in the Ohio Story.* Cleveland, OH: World Publishing Company, 1953.

Stephen, Leslie, and Sidney Lee, eds. *The Dictionary of National Biography.* Vol 2. London: Oxford University Press, 1921.

Terry, Thomas P. *Great Lakes Treasure Wrecks Atlas.* La Crosse, WI: Specialty Products, 1974.

Government Documents

Commonwealth of Pennsylvania. *Official Documents Comprising the Department and Other Reports Made to the Governor, Senate and House of Representatives of Pennsylvania.* Vol. 4. Harrisburg, PA: C.E Aughinbaugh, 1910.

Daugherty, H.M., and U.S. Congress. Senate. 68th Cong. 1st sess. *Litigation of Hon. Harry M. Daugherty, Formerly Attorney General of the United States.* Washington, D.C.: Government Printing Office, 1924.

Federal Bureau of Investigation. "John Dillinger." 62-29777. Section 2. Serials 31–59.

Journals

Bennett, Pamela J., and Richard A. Misselhorn, eds. "Curtis R. Burke's Civil War Journal." *Indiana Magazine of History* 65, no. 4 (December 1969): 283–327.

Forbes, John. "Letters of Gen. John Forbes, 1758." *Pennsylvania Magazine of History and Biography* 33, no. 1 (1909): 86–98.

Furlong, Patrick J. "Problems of Frontier Logistics in St. Clair's 1791 Campaign." Selected Papers from the 1983 and 1984 George Rogers Clark Trans-Appalachian Frontier History Conferences. npshistory.com/series/symposia/george_rogers_clark/1983-1984/sec6.htm.

Giddens, Paul H. "The Co-operation of the Southern Colonies in the Forbes Expedition Against Fort Duquesne." *Virginia Magazine of History and Biography* 36, no. 1 (January 1928): 1–16.

Griffenhagen, George. "Medicinal Liquor in the United States." *Pharmacy in History* 29, no. 1 (1987): 29–34.

Kent, Donald H. "The French Occupy the Ohio Country." *Pennsylvania History: A Journal of Mid-Atlantic Studies* 21, no. 4 (October 1954): 301–15.

King, R.S. "Silver Mines of Ohio Indians." *Ohio Archaeological and Historical Society Quarterly* 26, no. 1 (January 1917): 114–16.

Martin, David A. "The Changing Role of Foreign Money in the United States, 1782–1857." *Journal of Economic History* 37, no. 4 (December 1977): 1009–27.

Martin, Ronald D. "Confrontation at the Monongahela: Climax of the French Drive into the Upper Ohio Region." *Journal of Economic History* 37, no. 4 (December 1977): 133–50.

Miller, William Marion. "Major George W. Rue, the Captor of General John Morgan." *Ohio History Journal* 50, no. 2 (April–June 1941): 130–34.

———. "An Unrecorded Incident of Morgan's Raid." *Ohio History Journal* 70. No. 3 (July 1961): 244–45.

Moogk, Peter N. "When Money Talks: Coinage in New France." *Proceedings of the Meeting of the French Colonial Historical Society* 12 (1988): 69–105.

Mullen, Patrick B. "The Folk Idea of Unlimited Good in American Buried Treasure Legends." *Journal of the Folklore Institute* 15, no. 3 (September–December 1978): 209–20.

Quisenberry, A.C. "History of Morgan's Men." *Register of Kentucky State Historical Society* 15, no. 45 (September 1917): 21, 23–46.

Rockenbach, Stephen. "This Just Hope of Ultimate Payment: The Indiana Morgan's Raid Claims Commission and Harrison County, Indiana, 1863–1887." *Indiana Magazine of History* 109, no. 1 (March 2013): 45–60.

Roth, Mitchel. "Cholera, Community, and Public Health in Gold Rush Sacramento and San Francisco." *Pacific Historical Review* 66, no. 4 (November 1997): 527–51.

Rue, George W. "Celebration of the Surrender of General John H. Morgan." *Ohio History Journal* 20, no. 4 (October 1911): 368–77.

Toner, Joseph Meredith. "Washington in the Forbes Expedition of 1758." *Records of the Columbia Historical Society, Washington, D.C.* 1 (1897): 185–213.

Vance, Lee J. "Three Lessons in Rhabdomancy." *Journal of American Folk-Lore* 4, no. 14 (July–September 1891): 241–46.

Walker, Ronald W. "The Persisting Idea of American Treasure Hunting." *Brigham Young University Studies* 24, no. 4 (Fall 1984): 429–59.

Weber, L.J. "Morgan's Raid." *Ohio Archaeological and Historical Quarterly* 18, no. 1 (January 1909): 79–104.

Williams, Frank B., Jr. "893 Barrels of Jack Daniel's Old No. 7: The Troubles and Trials of Lem Motlow, 1923–1930." *Tennessee Historical Quarterly* 58, no. 1 (Spring 1999): 34–51.

Magazines and Newsletters

"The Buried Treasure Racket." *Popular Mechanics*, February 1937.

Chenoweth, Mary. "Inside Story of George Remus—'Bootleg King.'" *True Detective Magazine*, February 1929.

"Dillinger's Brain—Harry Pierpont." *Crime Does Not Pay*, December 1969.

"This Date in Dayton Diggers History, August 15th, 2009." *Digger's Gazette*, Fall 2015.

Newspapers

American Issue (Westerville, OH)

Aylmer Sun (Ontario, Canada)

Beecher (Michigan City, IN)

Canton Daily News (OH)

Canton Morning News (OH)

Chicago Tribune (IL)

Cincinnati Enquirer (OH)

Cleveland Daily Herald (OH)

Cleveland Leader (OH)
Cleveland Plain Dealer/Plain Dealer (OH)
Daily Journal (Delaware, OH)
Daily Union (Sacramento, CA)
Detroit Times (MI)
Enterprise (Wellington, OH)
Evening Star (Washington, D.C.)
Happner Gazette (OR)
Indianapolis Times/Indianapolis Daily Times (IN)
Lake County Times (Hammond, IN)
Mansfield Herald (OH)
Marietta Daily Leader (OH)
Marion Daily Mirror (OH)
National Intelligencer (Washington, D.C.)
News-Herald (Hillsboro, OH)
New York Times (NY)
Ohio Star (Ravenna, OH)
Perrysburg Journal (OH)
Pontiac Jacksonian (MI)
Port Stanley Beacon (Ontario, Canada)
Richland Shield and Banner (Mansfield, OH)
Ripley Bee (OH)
San Francisco Call (CA)
Spirit of Democracy (Woodsfield, OH)
Stark County Democrat (Canton, OH)
St. Louis Globe-Democrat (MO)
Washington Times (Washington, D.C.)
Watertown Leader (WI)

Online Sources

Bell, William. "Reno Gang's Reign of Terror." *Wild West Magazine*. February 2004. Posted to HistoryNet.com June 12, 2006. www.historynet.com/reno-gangs-reign-of-terror.

Botos, Tim. "Stark Heritage: Meyer Family, Part 1." *The Repository*. May 22, 2017. www.cantonrep.com/story/news/local/canton/2017/05/22/stark-heritage-meyer-family-part/20822285007.

———. "Stark Heritage Part 3: Andrew Meyer Family, Legends of Local Buried Treasures Never Uncovered." *The Repository*, May 23, 2017. www.cantonrep.com/story/news/local/canton/2017/05/23/stark-heritage-part-3-andrew/20814955007.

Collman, Ashley. "Couple Discover 1950s Suitcase Packed with $23,000 Hidden in the Walls of Their Home While Doing Renovations." *Daily Mail*, October 19, 2016. www.dailymail.co.uk/news/article-3852652/Couple-discover-1950s-suitcase-packed-23-000-hidden-walls-home-doing-renovations.html.

Haasnoot, Cory. "9 Lost Treasures of Ohio." Updated September 9, 2022. treasureseekr.com/lost-treasures-of-ohio.

Hand, Greg. "Hidden Cincinnati Treasure: Where Did Miles Ogle Bury the Cash?" *Cincinnati Curiosities*. tumblr. handeaux.tumblr.com/post/127858930077/hidden-cincinnati-treasure-where-did-miles-ogle.

"Intendant." *The Canadian Encyclopedia*. www.thecanadianencyclopedia.ca/en/article/intendant.

National Park Service. Fort Necessity National Battlefield. "Tanaghrisson, the Half King." www.nps.gov/people/tanaghrisson-the-half-king.htm.

Ohio History Center. "Logstown." ohiohistorycentral.org/w/Logstown.

———. "St. Clair's Defeat." ohiohistorycentral.org/w/St._Clair%27s_Defeat.

Poulsen, Ellen, and William J. Helmer. "Anna Sage: The Woman in Red." www.dillingerswomen.com/Anna-Sage.html.

Sinnott, John P. "Major General Braddock's March on Fort Duquesne." *Warfare History Network*. warfarehistorynetwork.com/major-general-braddocks-march-on-fort-duquesne.

Stoltz, Joseph F., III. "Jumonville Glen Skirmish." George Washington's Mount Vernon. www.mountvernon.org/library/digitalhistory/digital-encyclopedia/article/jumonville-glen-skirmish.

Stoner, Andrew E. "Dillinger, Denial, and Devotion: The Trials of Lena and Gilbert Pierpont." Indiana History Blog. December 10, 2021. blog.history.in.gov/author/andrew-e.

Veach, Michael R. "Bonded Warehouses." bourbonveach.com/2019/09/09/bonded-warehouses.

INDEX

ABOUT THE AUTHOR

Mark Strecker has wanted to be a writer since he first learned to read. He graduated from Bowling Green State University with a bachelor of arts degree in history in 1994 and a master's degree in library science from Clarion University in 2008, earning the latter to give him the skills needed to write well-researched narrative history. His greatest passions are history (no surprise there), travel, reading and comic book collecting. On his website, www.markstrecker.com, he posts original articles and travel logs about the various historic sites and museums he's visited. He lives in Ohio with a cat.

Visit us at
www.historypress.com